Student  **1A** Book

Apple Pie

Delta's Beginning ESL Program

Sadae Iwataki, Editor

Jean Owensby

Constance Turner

Greta Kojima

Joanne Abing

Jayme Adelson–Goldstein

REVISED EDITION

© 1993 by Delta Systems Co., Inc.
Revised Edition 1995

ISBN 0-937354-56-2

Production Staff:	Geoff Hill
	Diane Bergeron
	Linda Bruell
	Jeannie Patchin
Cover Design:	Geoff Hill
Illustrations:	Jim Ruskowski
	Brian Asimor
	Donna Lewis
	Laura Heuer

Delta Systems Co., Inc.
1400 Miller Parkway
McHenry, IL 60050 U.S.A.

Apple Pie 1A
Table of Contents

Communication Objectives:
Identify places in the community
Ask and answer questions about where people are

New Structures:
Prepositions of place *at, by*
Adverbs *here, there, over there*

Communication Objectives:
Identify everyday items carried in pockets or handbags
Describe locations of items
Help someone find a lost item

New Structure:
Prepositions of place *in, on, under*

Communication Objectives:
Identify appliances and places in a kitchen
Give and follow instructions
Identify furniture in a living room

New Structure:
Preposition of place *next to*

Unit One

New Class, New Friends

Hi! I'm Tony

Objectives: In this lesson you will learn how to introduce yourself, ask and answer questions about names, and follow simple directions.

Something New: Classroom Directions

Listen

Hello, class.
Hello, students.

My name's *Mrs. Baker*.
I'm *Mrs. Baker*.

Repeat

Hello, *Mrs. Baker*.

Answer

Hello, class!
Hello, *Mrs. Baker!*

What's my name?
(It's) *Mrs. Baker*.

What's your name?
(It's) *Maria Diaz*.
(It's) *Ken Wong*.

Let's Talk: Hi! I'm Tony

Tony: Hi! I'm Tony.
May: Hello! I'm May.
Tony: Nice to meet you.
May: Nice to meet you, too.

☞ Practice: "Hi! I'm Tony"

1. Tony: Hi! I'm Tony.
2. Yuki: Hi! I'm Yuki.
3. Rosa: Hi! I'm Rosa.

☞ Practice: "Nice to meet you"

4. Student 1: Hi! I'm *Ben*.
   Student 2: Hi! I'm *Lisa*.

   S1: Nice to meet you.
   S2: Nice to meet you, too.

5. Student 1: Hello, my name's *Maria*.
   Student 2: Hello, I'm *Jenny*.

   S1: Nice to meet you.
   S2: Nice to meet you, too.

★ Something Extra

You can also say: "It's nice to meet you."
"I'm happy to meet you."
"I'm glad to meet you."

Let's Talk: What's Your Last Name?

May: Tony, what's your last name?

Tony: (It's) Vega. What's your last name?

May: (It's) Lei.

Tony: Lei? Is your name May Lei?

May: Yes. My first name's May and my last name's Lei.

☛ **Practice: "What's your first name?"**

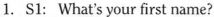

1. S1: What's your first name?
   S2: My first name's Lisa.
   S1: What's your last name?
   S2: My last name's Leiva.

2. S1: What's your first name?
   S2: (It's) Sook.
   S1: What's your last name?
   S2: (It's) Kim.

■ Interaction

1. Walk around the room.
2. Talk to a partner.

   Example: S1: Hi, I'm *Ken*. What's your name?

   S2: My name's *Maria*. What's your last name?

   S1: *Vega*. What's your last name?

   S2: *Diaz*.

   S1: Nice to meet you.

   S2: Nice to meet you, too.

3. Talk to another partner.

Reading and Writing: The Alphabet

Capital (big) Letters

A B C D E F G H I
J K L M N O P Q R
S T U V W X Y Z

A B C D E F G H I J K L M
N O P Q R S T U V W X Y Z

Small Letters

a b c d e f g h i
j k l m n o p q r
s t u v w x y z

a b c d e f g h i j k l m
n o p q r s t u v w x y z

☛ Practice: "Spell your name"

1. LISTEN to the alphabet.
2. REPEAT the alphabet.
3. SAY the letters of the alphabet.
4. SPELL your first name.
5. SPELL your last name.

☛ Practice Activity: Print your name

1. Print your first name.
2. Print your last name.
3. Talk to a partner.
4. Write your partner's first and last name.

My Name	My Partner's Name
_____	_____
First	First
_____	_____
Last	Last

☛ Practice Activity: Name cards

1. Print your first name on the card.
2. Print your last name on the card.
3. Show your card and read your name.

Lesson 1 Activity Page

A. Look!

Make a circle.

Write a letter.

Circle the letter.

B. Read and do it!

1. Make a circle.

2. Write a letter.

3. Circle the letter.

B

4. Circle the first name.

Joe Sanchez

Anh Tran

Yuki Ohara

5. Circle the last name.

Sue Kim

Cesar Castro

Hector Ortega

6. Read the question. Circle the letter of the answer.
   a. Nice to meet you.
   b. Susan Davis.
   c. Hello, students.

What's your name?

7. Read the answer. Circle the letter of the question.
   a. What's your first name?
   b. Hello, class.
   c. What's your last name?

Davis

Lesson 2

Touch the Floor

Objectives: In this lesson you will learn to follow simple directions, name classroom objects, and introduce friends.

✔ Review

Name Cards

1. Show your name card.
2. Read your name.

    Example: My name's *Tony Vega*.

    My first name's *Tony*.

    My last name's *Vega*.
3. Spell your name.

    Example: T – O – N – Y   V – E – G – A

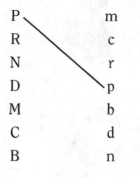

The Alphabet

Match the letters.

P	m		A	v
R	c		S	e
N	r		F	a
D	p		V	l
M	b		W	s
C	d		E	w
B	n		L	f

Something New: Classroom Objects
Listen and Look

pen   pencil   book   notebook

chair   desk   clock   chalkboard

window   door   flag   wall

☛ Practice: "It's a window"

1. S1: What's this?
   S2: It's a window.

2. S1: What's this?
   S2: It's a chair.

Something New: Following Directions

Touch	chair	desk	pencil
Hold up	pen	book	notebook
Put down	pen	book	notebook
Point to	window	door	chalkboard
Show me	clock	pencil	flag

☛ **Practice Activity: Point to the flag**

1. S1: Point to the flag.
   S2: (Points to the flag)

2. S1: Hold up a pen.
   S2: (Holds up a pen)

3. S1: Put down the pen.
   S2: (Puts down the pen)

4. S1: Touch a notebook.
   S2: (Touches a notebook)

5. S1: Point to the clock.
   S2: (Points to the clock)

6. S1: Hold up a book.
   S2: (Holds up a book)

Let's Talk: This Is My Friend Sara

May: Mrs. Baker, this is my friend Sara Gomez.
Sara, this is Mrs. Baker.

Mrs. Baker: I'm glad to meet you, Sara.

Sara: I'm happy to meet you, Mrs. Baker.

☛ Practice: "This is my friend"

May: Sara, this is my friend Tony.
Tony, this is Sara.

Tony: I'm happy to meet you, Sara.

Sara: I'm happy to meet you, too.

Note: You can also say:

"How do you do? I'm happy to meet you."
or
"How do you do? I'm glad to meet you."

☛ Practice Activity: Meeting other students

1. Show the class your name card.
2. Introduce yourself.
   Example: My name's *Tony Vega*.
3. Choose a partner.
4. Introduce your partner to the class.
   Example: This is my friend *Rosa*.

Reading: A New Student

Sara Maria Gomez

Sara Gomez is a new student. Her middle name is Maria. Her full name is Sara Maria Gomez.

Circle the correct answer.

1. Maria is her first name.   yes   no
2. Gomez is her last name.   yes   no
3. She's a new student.   yes   no
4. Her middle name is Sara.   yes   no

✍ **Writing:** The Alphabet (Cursive)
Capital (big) letters

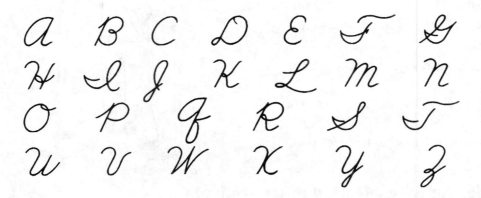

Small letters

$a\ b\ c\ d\ e\ f\ g\ h\ i\ j\ k\ l\ m$
$n\ o\ p\ q\ r\ s\ t\ u\ v\ w\ x\ y\ z$

1. Copy the capital letters of the alphabet in your notebook.

2. Copy the small letters of the alphabet in your notebook.

3. Print your full name: _____

4. Sign your full name: _____

Lesson 2 Activity Pages

A. *Listen to the spelling. Write the name.*

Henry
Gina
Eliza
John
Chris
Vera

1. *Eliza* _____
2. _____
3. _____
4. _____
5. _____
6. _____

B. *Look and read.*

> *What's your name?*

Copy the question.

_____

Answer the question.

_____

C. *Write.*

1. Write your first name: _____

2. Write your last name: _____

3. Copy the question: *What's your name?* _____

4. Answer the question: *What's your name?* _____

D. Listen and write.

1.

chair

2.

notebook

3.

pencil

4.

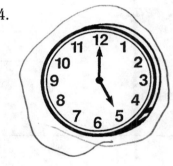

clock

5.

window

6.

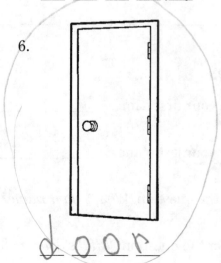

door

E. Say the word. Spell the word. Circle the picture. Write the word.

1. chair _____

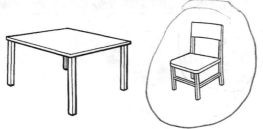

2. pen _____

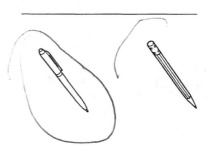

3. pencil _____

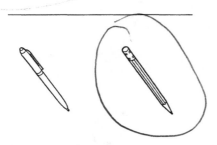

4. alphabet _____

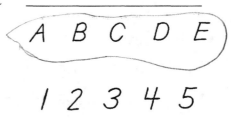

5. book _____

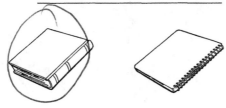

6. table _____

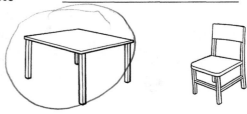

7. window _____

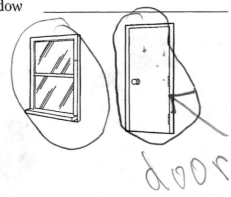

door

8. notebook _____

write in a
notebook

How Are You Today?

Objectives: In this lesson you will learn to greet friends, say how you feel, and say goodbye.

✔ Review
The Alphabet (Cursive)

1. Write the missing letters, capital or small.

Capital	Small		Capital	Small
$\mathcal{a}$	___		___	m
$\mathcal{H}$	___		$\mathcal{Y}$	___
___	s		$\mathcal{q}$	___
$\mathcal{G}$	___		___	c
$\mathcal{R}$	___		___	b
___	x		___	w
___	j		$\mathcal{E}$	___

2. Now say the letters.

Following Directions

Follow the teacher's directions:

Touch
Point to
Hold up
Put down
Show me

Something New: How Are You Today?
Listen and Look

fine

okay

Let's Talk: I'm Fine, Thanks

Tony: Hi, May. How are you today?
May: I'm fine, thanks. And you?
Tony: Okay.

☛ Practice: "I'm fine"

1. S1: How are you today?
   S2: I'm fine, thanks.

2. S1: How are you today?
   S2: I'm okay.

■ **Interaction:** Hi Sara, How Are You?

1. Walk around the room.
2. Greet four friends by name.
3. Ask how they are today.
4. Answer their questions.

Let's Talk: Bye, Tony

Class is over now. The students are leaving the room.

May: Bye, Tony.
Tony: So long, May.
      See you tomorrow.
May: So long.

★ **Something Extra:** Saying Goodbye

Bye.	So long.	See you.
Goodbye.	See you later.	See you tomorrow.

☞ **Practice: "So long, Maria"**

1. S1: So long, Maria.
   S2: See you later.

2. S1: Goodbye, Mrs. Baker.
   S2: Goodbye, May.

■ Interaction: Hello and Goodbye

1. Walk around the room.
2. Practice saying hello and goodbye.

Examples: S1: Hi, how are you?
S2: Hello. I'm fine.

S1: Bye. See you tomorrow.
S2: So long.

Reading: Greetings

I go to work. I see my friends. I say, "Hi! How are you?" When work is over, I say, "Bye. See you tomorrow."

Discussion

1. What do you say when you see friends?
2. What do you say when you say goodbye?
3. What do you say to your family when you leave home?

✍ Writing

Write the correct words on the lines.

1. How are you today?

   _____

2. _____

   See you later.

Nice to meet you.
I'm okay.
So long.

Lesson 3 Activity Pages

A. Read and write.

happy	I'm	is	meet	Nice

1. Hi, _____ Tony.

_____ to meet you, Tony.

2. Tony, this _____ my friend May.

I'm _____ to meet you, May.

I'm happy to _____ you, too.

B. Copy the letters.

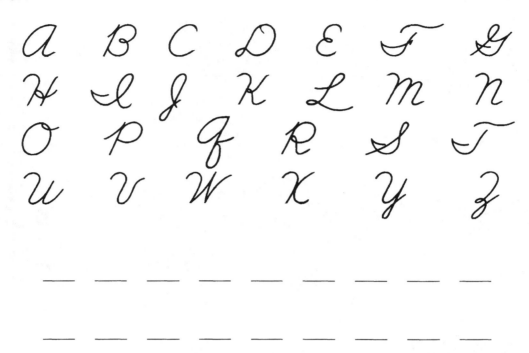

$A \quad B \quad C \quad D \quad E \quad F \quad G$
$H \quad I \quad J \quad K \quad L \quad M \quad N$
$O \quad P \quad Q \quad R \quad S \quad T$
$U \quad V \quad W \quad X \quad Y \quad Z$

- - - - - - - -

- - - - - - - -

- - - - - - - -

$a \quad b \quad c \quad d \quad e \quad f \quad g \quad h \quad i \quad j \quad k \quad l \quad m$
$n \quad o \quad p \quad q \quad r \quad s \quad t \quad u \quad v \quad w \quad x \quad y \quad z$

- - - - - - - -

- - - - - - - -

- - - - - - - -

C. Read, copy and do it.

Work with a friend.

1. Touch a pencil. _____

2. Hold up a book. _____

3. Show me a pen. _____

4. Point to a window. _____

5. Put down the pencil. _____

Unit One  Evaluation

Sample Exercise

I. Listening Comprehension

Listen to the teacher.

Circle the correct answer, A or B.

[Teacher: It's a table.]

 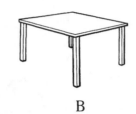

A   B

Answer: B is correct/right.

A is incorrect/wrong.

II. Reading

Circle the correct answer.

It's a _____ .

door   first   fine

Answer: (door)   first   fine

III. Writing

Choose the correct word and write it on the line.

1. I'm _____ to meet you.

2. How _____ you?

Answers: 1. glad
2. are

are
glad
nice
student

I. Listening Comprehension

Listen to the teacher.

Circle the correct answer, A or B.

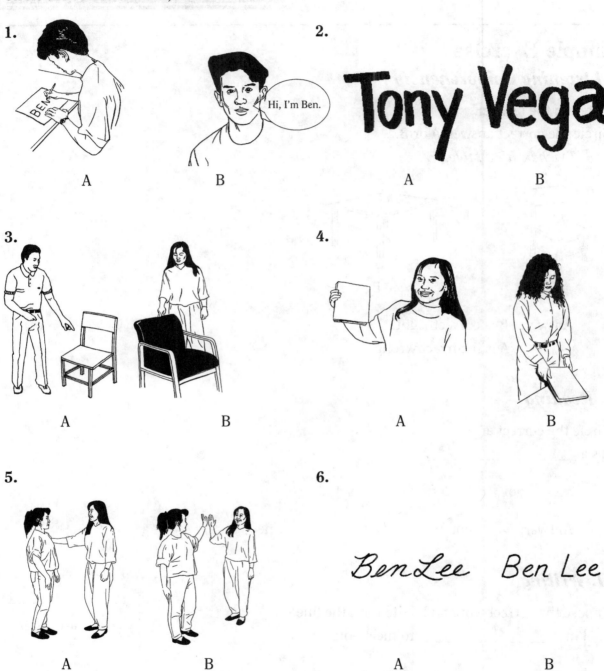

1.

A   B

2.

A   B

3.

A   B

4.

A   B

5.

A   B

6.

A   B

II. Reading

Circle the correct answer.

1. What's your _____ ?

   last   name   first

2. _____ name's May.

   It's   I'm   My

3. Hold up a _____ .

   door   pencil   chalkboard

4. See _____ tomorrow.

   my   your   you

III. Writing

Choose the correct word and write it on the line.

1. _____ to meet you.

2. What's your _____ name?

3. I'm _____ , thank you.

4. _____ me a notebook.

5. _____ a window.

fine
first
It's
Nice
Put
Sara
Show
What's

Notes

Unit Two

Numbers

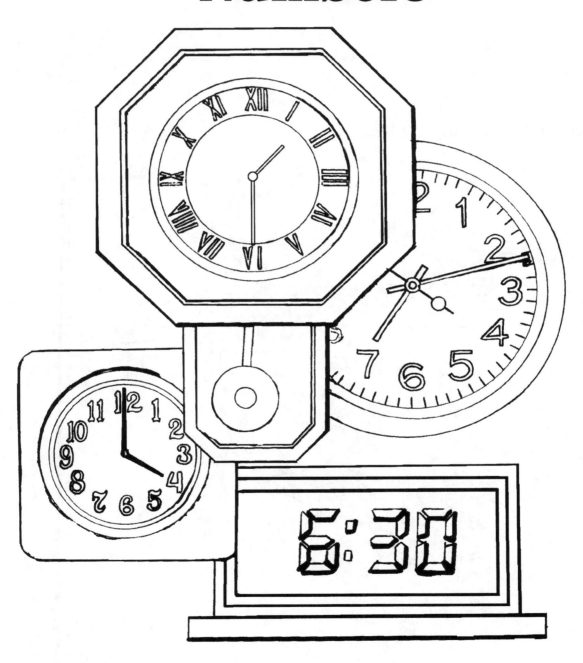

What's Your Address?

Objectives: In this lesson you will learn numbers from 1 to 12, and to ask and answer questions about someone's address and phone number.

✔ **Review:** Our Classroom

Something New: Numbers
Listen and Look

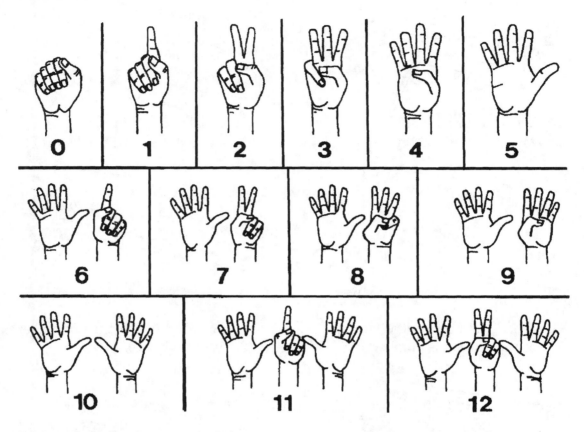

Let's Talk: What's Your Address?

Ben Lee is a new student. He is in the school office. The clerk is helping him with the registration form.

Clerk: What's your address?

Ben: (My address is) 104 Fay Street.

Clerk: What's your city?

Ben: (My city's) Los Angeles.

Clerk: What's your zip code?

Ben: (My zip code's) 90018.

Clerk: What's your phone number?

Ben: It's 555–6370.

☛ **Practice: "My address is 109 Union Avenue"**

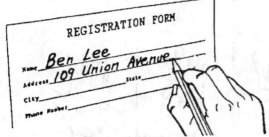

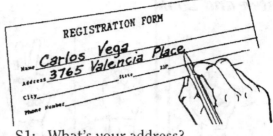

1. S1: What's your address?
   S2: My address is 109 Union Avenue.

2. S1: What's your address?
   S2: My address is 3765 Valencia Place.

3. S1: What's your apartment number?
   S2: My apartment is number 5.

4. S1: What's your apartment number?
   S2: It's number 202.

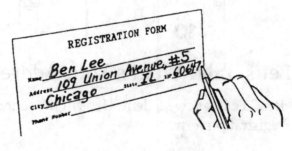

5. S1: What's your city?
   S2: My city's Chicago.

6. S1: What's your zip code?
   S2: My zip code's 60647.

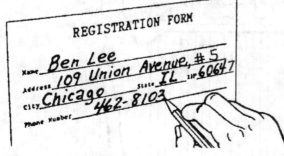

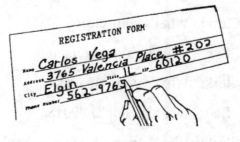

7. S1: What's your phone number?
   S2: My phone number is 462–8103.

8. S1: What's your phone number?
   S2: It's 562–9765.

★ Something Extra: Area Codes for Telephones

Area codes for some cities in the United States:

Chicago	312	Miami	305
El Paso	915	New York City	212
Los Angeles	213	Seattle	206

Your city _____ Area Code _____

Call a friend in Chicago. The telephone number is 322–6571.

Dial 1 + area code + telephone number

1 + 312 + 322–6571

Call a friend in Miami. The telephone number is 447–6129.

Dial 1 + area code + telephone number

1 + 305 + 447–6129

Call a friend:

City	Phone number	1 + area code + phone number
Los Angeles	462–8103	1 + 213 + _____
El Paso	829–3406	1 + _____
Seattle	951–4075	_____
New York City	755–1842	_____
_____	_____	_____
_____	_____	_____

Something New: State Abbreviations

Look at the map. Draw a line from the abbreviations to the states.

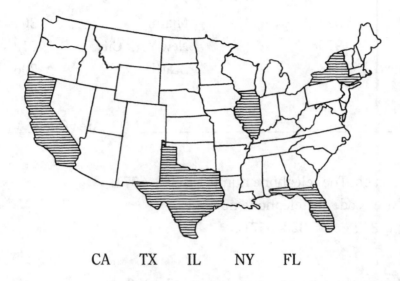

CA   TX   IL   NY   FL

What is the abbreviation for your state? _____

■ Interaction: Address Book

1. This is your new address book. Write your name and address.
2. Ask two students, "Please write your name and address."

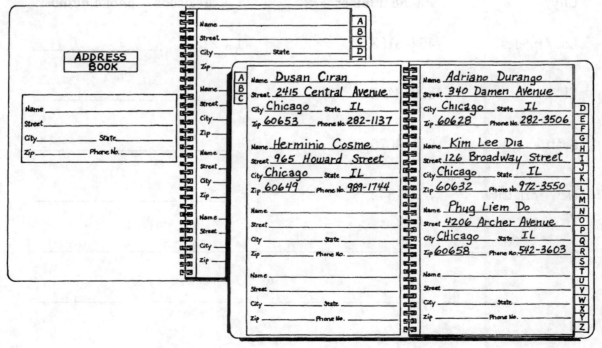

★ Something Extra: Commas

When you write the city and state for an address, use three steps:

1. Write the city name.
2. Put a comma.
3. Write the state abbreviation.

Examples: Los Angeles, CA

New York, NY

Miami, FL

Houston, TX

Chicago, IL

☛ Practice Activity: A letter to a friend

This is an envelope. It is your letter to a friend. Write your return address on the envelope. Write a friend's name and address on the envelope. (Look at your address book on page 32.)

Your name

Your address

Your city, state and zip code

Your friend's name

Your friend's address

Your friend's city, state and zip code

Reading: Ruben's Letter to a Friend

My name is Ruben Silva. My address is 167 Olympic Boulevard. My city is Los Angeles. My state is California. My zip code is 90013.

My friend's name is Lan Yee. Her address is 851 Benton Drive. Her city is Chicago, and her state is Illinois. Her zip code is 60641.

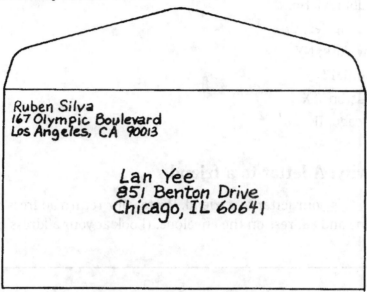

Discussion

1. Who is sending the letter? What is his address?
2. Who is receiving the letter? What is her address?
3. Do you send letters to friends in the U.S.?
   What's the city? What's the state? What's the zip code?

✍ **Writing**

1. What's your last _____ ?

   My last name's _____ .

2. _____ your zip code?

   My zip code's _____ .

3. What's your _____ ?

   My city's _____ .

city
It's
name
90013
Los Angeles
Silva
What's

Lesson 4 Activity Page

A. Listen and write the missing information.

Name	Address	City	State	Zip code
1. Paul Smith	_____ Pine St.	Houston	TX	_____
2. Yuki Ohara	_____ Grand Ave.	Los Angeles	CA	_____
3. Sunay Kim	_____ 5th Ave.	New York	NY	_____
4. Henry Lee	_____ Elm Blvd.	Seattle	WA	_____

B. Read and do it.

1. Print your name. _____

2. Sign your name. _____

C. Read the directions. Fill in the form.

Directions: Print your information on lines 1, 2 and 3.
Sign your name on line 4.

1. _____
   LAST NAME   FIRST NAME   MIDDLE NAME

2. _____
   NUMBER   STREET   APARTMENT NO.

3. _____
   CITY   STATE   ZIP CODE

4. _____
   SIGNATURE

What Time Is It?

Objectives: In this lesson you will learn polite expressions and ask and answer questions about time.

✔ Review: Numbers

Listen to the teacher. Fill in the numbers.

1. _____ Fletcher Drive

2. _____ books

3. _____ pencils

4. _____ windows

5. My zip code is _____ .

6. _____ Rush Street

7. The school telephone number is

_____ .

Something New: Telling Time
Listen and Look

Let's Talk: What Time Is It?

Sara is at the bus stop. She is going to work.

Sara:	Excuse me. What time is it?
Mrs. Green:	It's 6 o'clock.
Sara:	Thank you.
Mrs. Green:	You're welcome.

☛ **Practice: "What time is it?"**

1. S1: Excuse me. What time is it?

   S2: It's - - - - - - - - - - - - - - - - - .

3. S1: Excuse me. What time is it?

   S2: It's - - - - - - - - - - - - - - - - .

   S1: Thank you.

   S2: You're welcome.

2. S1: Pardon me. What time is it?

   S2: It's - - - - - - - - - - - - - - - - - .

4. S1: Pardon me. What time is it?

   S2: - - - - - - - - - - - - - 9 o'clock.

   S1: Thanks.

   S2: You're welcome.

Something New: Greetings

Luis: Good morning, Maria.
Maria: Good morning, Luis.

Thanh Ly: Good afternoon, Jose.
Jose: Good afternoon, Thanh Ly.

Sue: Good evening, Mrs. Baker.
Mrs. Baker: Good evening, Sue.

Good night

☞ Practice: "It's 10 o'clock"

1. S1:   Good morning.
   S2:   Good morning. What time is it?
   S1:   It's 10 o'clock.

2. S1:   Good afternoon.
   S2:   Good afternoon. What time is it?
   S1:   It's 3 o'clock.

3. S1:   Good evening.
   S2:   Good evening. What time is it?
   S1:   It's 8 o'clock.

Something New: It's 1:30

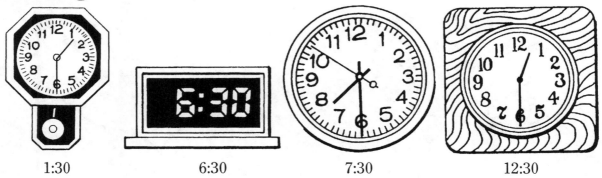

1:30　　　　　　6:30　　　　　7:30　　　　　12:30

☞ Practice: "It's 3:30"

1. S1: What time is it?　　　　2. S1: What time is it?
   S2: It's 3:30.　　　　　　　　　S2: It's 9:30.

Reading: Good Morning, Ben

Bob Lewis: Good morning, Ben.

Ben Tran: Good morning, Bob.

Mr. Green: Excuse me. What time is it?

Bob Lewis: I'm sorry. I don't know.

Ben Tran: It's 8:30.

Mr. Green: Thank you.

Ben Tran: You're welcome.

☞ **Practice: "I'm sorry. I don't know"**

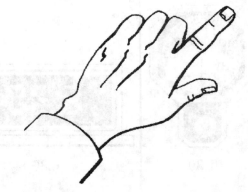

1. S1: What time is it?
   S2: It's 7:30.

2. S1: What time is it?
   S2: I'm sorry. I don't know.

✍ **Writing**

1. Excuse me. What time is it?

   _____ .

2. Is it 3:30?

   _____ , it _____ .

3. What _____ ?

   It's 6:30.

   _____ .

   You're welcome.

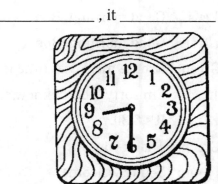

4. What time is it?

   _____ .

   Thank you.

   _____ .

Lesson 5 Activity Pages

A. Listen. Circle the correct letter.

1.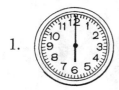

    a.   b.   c.

2.

    a.   b.   c.

3.

    a.   b.   c.

4.

    a.   b.   c.

5. It's 6 o'clock.   It's 6:30.   It's 7:30.

    a.   b.   c.

6. It's 9 o'clock.   It's 6:30.   It's 9:30.

    a.   b.   c.

B. Read the time. Draw the hands on the clock.

1. It's 2:00.    2. It's 6:00.    3. It's 12:00.

4. It's 1:30.    5. It's 4:30.    6. It's 9:30.

C. Look at the picture and write the greeting.

1. _____

2. _____

3. _____

4. _____

5. _____

6. _____

D. Work with a partner.

Look at the picture and write the time.

What Time Is It?

Your opinion   *Your partner's opinion*

1. _____   _____

2. _____   _____

3. _____   _____

4. _____   _____

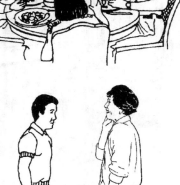

5. _____   _____

I'm Sorry I'm Late

Objectives: In this lesson you will learn to apologize for being late. You will also learn to say good night.

✔ Review: Time

Use a practice clock. Ask each other the time.

> ***Example:*** S1 to S2: What time is it?
> S2: It's 7 o'clock.
> S2 to S3: What time is it?
> S3: It's 9 o'clock.

Something New: It's Early
Listen and Look

It's early.   It's late.

Let's Talk: I'm Sorry I'm Late

Sara: Oh, I'm late.
           What time is it?
Custodian: It's 7.

Sara: Good evening, Mrs. Baker.
           I'm sorry I'm late.
Mrs Baker: That's all right, Sara.
           We're on page 10.

Note: You can say "7 o'clock" or "7."

☛ Practice: "I'm early"

1. S1: I'm late. What time is it?
   S2: It's 7:30.

2. S1: I'm early. What time is it?
   S2: It's 6:00.

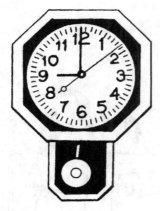

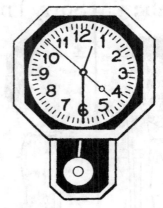

3. S1: What time is it?

   S2: It's - - - - - - - - - - .

   I'm sorry I'm late.

   S1: That's okay.

4. S1: What - - - - - - - - - - - ?

   S2: It's - - - - - - - - - - - .

   I'm - - - - - - - - - - - late.

   S1: That's - - - - - - - - - - - .

☞ **Practice: "That's okay"**

1. S1: I'm sorry - - - - - - - -

   - - - - - - - - - - - - - - .

   S2: That's okay.

2. S1: - - - - - - - - - - - -

   I'm late.

   S2: That's all right.

3. S1: - - - - - - - - - - - -

   - - - - - - - - - - - - .

   S2: - - - - - - - - - - - - .

Reading: Kim Is Early; Bob Is Late

Tony's party is at 8 o'clock. It's 7:30 now. Kim is early.

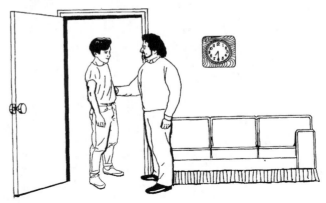

Kim: Hi, Tony.
Tony: Good evening, Kim.

Later, at 9:30 . . .

Bob: Hi, Tony. I'm sorry I'm late.
Tony: That's okay.

Yes or No

1. Kim is early.   yes   no
2. The party is at 7:30.   yes   no

3. Bob is late.   yes   no
4. It's in the morning.   yes   no

Let's Talk: Good Night, Kim

Tony's party is over. His friends are going home.

Kim: Great party, Tony. Good night.
Tony: Good night, Kim.
Bob: Thanks, Tony. Good night.
Tony: Good night, Bob.

☛ Practice: "Good evening, Tony"

1. S1: Good morning, Sara.
   S2: Good morning, Mia.

2. S1: Good evening, Tony.
   S2: - - - - - - - - - - -, Mark.

3. S1: Good night, Mark.
   S2: - - - - - - - - - - -, Tony.

✎ Writing

1. Is it 6:30?

   Yes, _____ .

2. _____ 5:00?

   Yes, _____ .

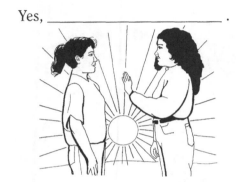

3. _____ , Mia.

4. _____ , Mark.

5. _____ , Thanh.

6. It's late. _____ , Octavio.

7. I'm sorry _____ .

   That's okay.

8. I'm sorry I'm late.

   _____ .

Lesson 6 Activity Pages

A. Talk about the picture.

B. Look at the picture. Read the questions and circle the answers.

1. Is it a classroom?   yes   no

2. Is it morning?   yes   no

3. Is it afternoon?   yes   no

4. Is it evening?   yes   no

5. Is it late?   yes   no

6. What time is it? _____

C. Read the story. Write the missing words.

7	8:00	is	sorry	I'm	is	okay	late

This is an ESL classroom. Mr. Stevens _____ the teacher and Oscar _____ a

student in room number _____ . It's _____ p.m. and Oscar

is _____ . Oscar is _____ he's late.

Oscar: Sorry _____ late Mr. Stevens.

Mr. Stevens: That's _____ , Oscar. Sit down.

Notes

Unit Two Evaluation

I. Listening Comprehension

Listen to the teacher.

Circle the correct answer, A or B.

1. A   B

2. A   B

3. A   B

4. A. Yes, it is.   B. No, it isn't.

5. A   B

6. A   B

7. A   B

8. A   B

II. Reading

Circle the correct answer.

1. My _____ Houston.
   name's   city's   zip code's

2. Excuse me. What _____ is it?
   time   five   clock

3. What's your _____ ?
   evening   phone number   o'clock

4. I'm sorry I'm _____ .
   early   late   time

III. Writing

Choose the correct word and write it on the line.

1. Good _____ , Jose.

2. What's your _____ ?

3. My city's _____ .

4. What _____ is it?

   It's 3 _____ .

5. I'm _____ I'm late.

6. Thank you.

   You're _____ .

city
evening
Miami
name's
o'clock
sorry
time
welcome

Unit Three

Meet Cooks, Doctors, and Homemakers

I'm a Doctor; She's a Doctor, Too

Objective: In this lesson you will learn to talk about someone's job.

✔ **Review:** It's Early/Late

Cover the right side of the page. Practice with the pictures first.

1.

What time is the movie?

What time is it now?

It's early/late.

2.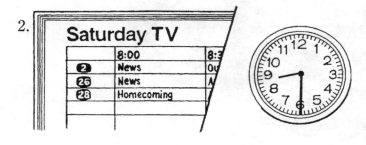

What time is the TV program?

What time is it now?

It's early/late.

3.

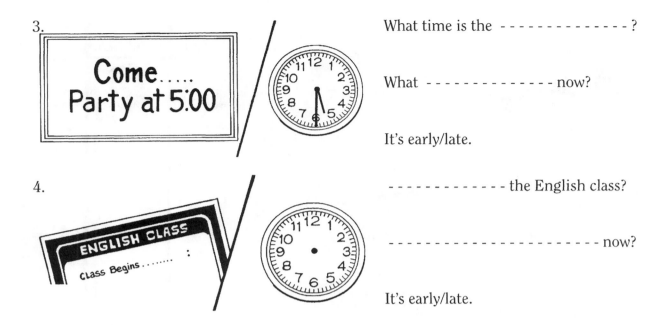

What time is the - - - - - - - - - - - - - ?

What - - - - - - - - - - - - - now?

It's early/late.

4.

- - - - - - - - - - - - the English class?

- now?

It's early/late.

Something New: Occupations
Listen and Look

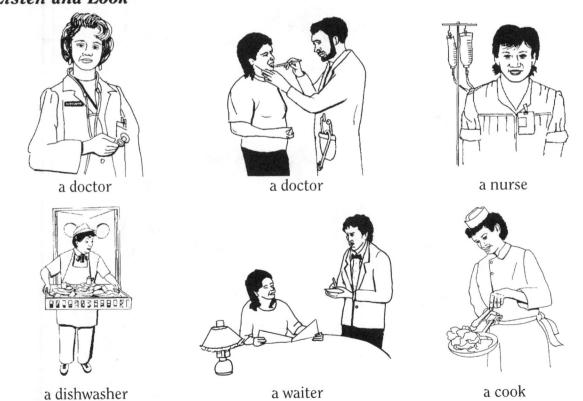

a doctor

a doctor

a nurse

a dishwasher

a waiter

a cook

a secretary

a homemaker

a salesclerk

a factory worker

a bus driver

a gardener

Let's Talk: He's a Doctor, Too

Sara is at the hospital with her husband Tomas. Sara sees many workers at the hospital.

Sara: Is she a nurse?
Tomas: No, she isn't.
She's a doctor.
Sara: And what is he?
Tomas: He's a doctor, too.

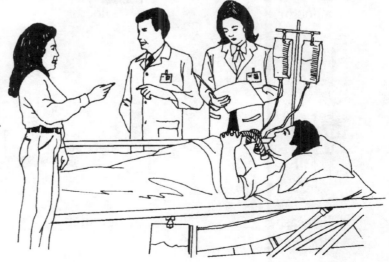

☞ **Practice: "Are you a student?"**

1. S1: Are you a student?
   S2: Yes, I am.

2. S1: Is she a secretary?
   S2: Yes, she is.

3. S1: Is he a waiter?
   S2: Yes, he is.

4. S1: Are you a teacher?
   S2: No, I am not.

5. S1: Is he a gardener?
   S2: No, he isn't.

6. S1: Is she a secretary?
   S2: No, she isn't.
      She's a nurse.

 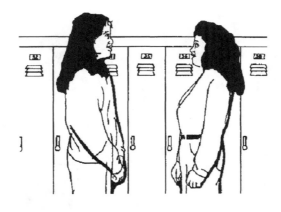 

7. S1: Is he a student?
   S2: No, he isn't.
   S1: What is he?
   S2: He's a salesclerk.

8. S1: Are you a new student?
   S2: Yes, - - - - - - - - - - - - - .
   S1: I - - - - - - - - - - - - , too.

9. S1: Is she a doctor?
   S2: No, she isn't.
   S1: - - - - - - - - - - she?
   S2: - - - - - - - - - - - .

☛ **Practice Activity: Talk about your job**

1. In a group, tell other students your job.
2. Practice with *I, You, He, She*.
3. Tell the class about your group.

Reading: The English Teacher

My name is June Baker. I am a teacher. This is room 2. It is an English class. Welcome to class!

Discussion

1. Is my name Sue Baker?
2. Am I a teacher or a student?
3. Is this Room 2 or 12?
4. Is this a Spanish class?
5. Are you a teacher or a student?
6. What's your classroom number?

✍ **Writing**

Write the question or answer.

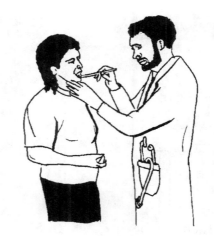

1. Is she a homemaker?

_____ .

2. Is he a nurse?

_____ .

3. _____ ?

Yes, she is.

4. Is she a homemaker?

No, she _____ .

5. _____

_____ ?

Yes, he is.

_____

6. Is he a cook?

_____ .

What is he?

_____ .

★ **Something Extra:** Your Occupation

Write about yourself. Give your name and occupation.

_____

_____

_____

_____

A. Write the word, copy it and circle the picture.

1. d o c t o r

   doctor

2. __ e __ c __ e __

3. __ __ c __ t __ y

4. __ a __ __ r

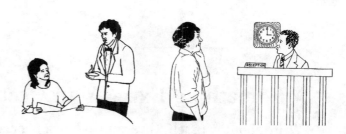

5. __ o __ __ k __

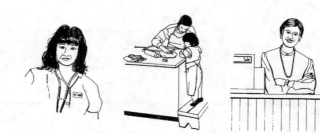

B. Write.

1. He's a _____ *salesclerk* _____ .

2. She's a _____ .

3. He's a _____ and

she's a _____ , too!

4. She's a _____ and

he's a _____ , too!

5. He's _____ and

_____ , too!

Lesson 8

Are You New Students?

Objective: In this lesson you will learn to ask and answer questions about people and their occupations.

✔ Review: Occupations

Draw a line from the worker to the place where he/she works.

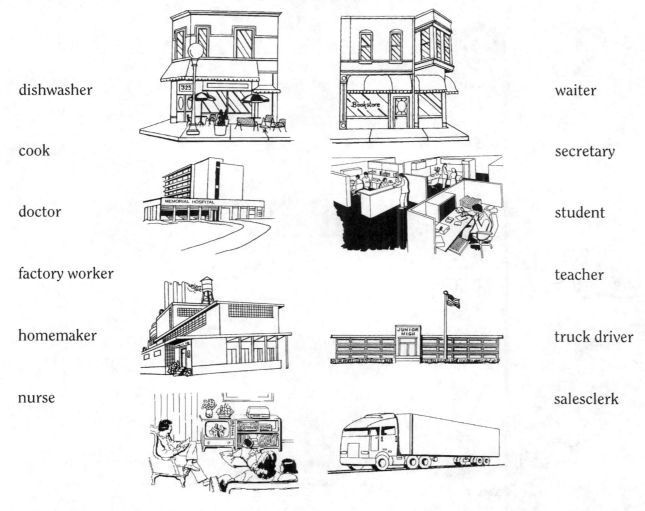

dishwasher

cook

doctor

factory worker

homemaker

nurse

waiter

secretary

student

teacher

truck driver

salesclerk

Something New: People and Occupations
Listen and Look

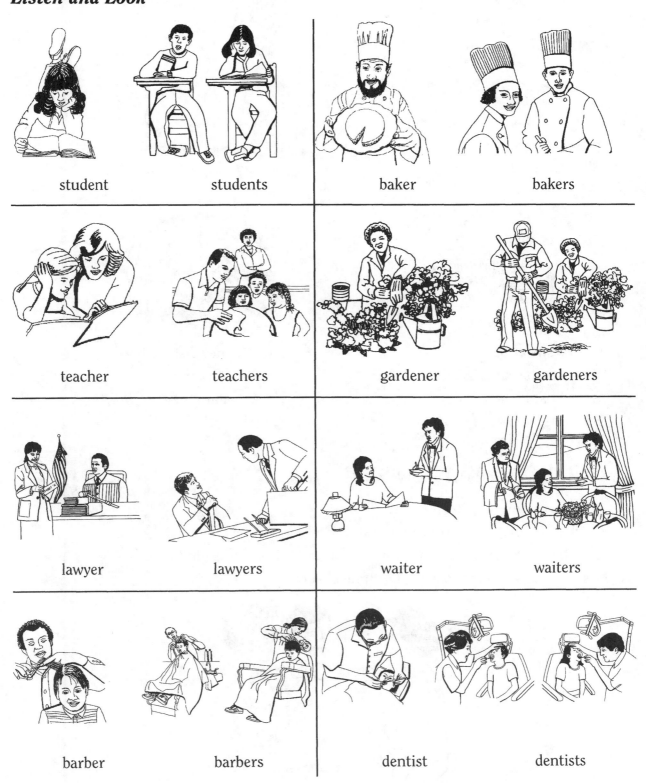

student	students	baker	bakers
teacher	teachers	gardener	gardeners
lawyer	lawyers	waiter	waiters
barber	barbers	dentist	dentists

☞ **Practice: "Are they bakers?"**

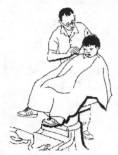

1. S1: Is he a barber?
   S2: Yes, he is.

2. S1: Are they bakers?
   S2: Yes, they are.

3. S1: Is she a teacher?
   S2: No, she isn't.
   S1: What is she?
   S2: She's a lawyer.

4. S1: Are they dishwashers?
   S2: No, they aren't.
   S1: What are they?
   S2: They're waiters.

Let's Talk: Are You New Students?

Maria: Are you the teacher?

Mrs. Baker: Yes, I am. Are you new students?

Victor: Yes, we are. I'm Victor Rivera, and this is my sister Maria.

Mrs. Baker: Welcome to class. I'm June Baker.

☛ Practice: "Are they barbers?"

1. S1: Are you a student?
   S2: Yes, I am.

2. S1: Are you students?
   S2: Yes, we are.

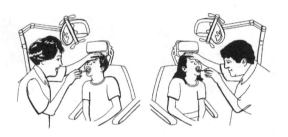

3. S1: Are they lawyers?
   S2: Yes, they are.

4. S1: Are they barbers?
   S2: No, they aren't.

5. S1: Are you waiters?
   S2: No, we aren't.

6. S1: Are you a dentist?
   S2: No, I'm not.

☛ Practice: "Contractions"

He's (He is)	a student.	We're (We are)	students.
She's (She is)	a dentist.	They're (They are)	waiters.
I'm (I am)	a lawyer.	You're (You are)	teachers.

☛ **Practice Activity: What's your job**

1. Tell each other your occupations.
2. Practice with *I'm, We're, You're, He's, She's, They're*.

Reading: Adult School Students

Sergio Macias is a busser and Carlos Lopez is a waiter in the daytime. At night they are students at Westside Adult School. There is an English class four evenings a week. There is no school on Fridays.

✍ Writing

1. Are Sergio Macias and Carlos Lopez restaurant workers?

   Yes, _____ .

   Sergio _____ and Carlos_____ .

2. Are they students, too?

   _____ .

3. Are they in school every evening?

   _____ .

4. Are you in school every evening?

   _____ .

5. Are they barbers?

   _____ .

6. Are they lawyers?

   _____ .

7. Are they doctors?

   _____ .

   What are they?

   _____ .

Lesson 8 Activity Pages

A. Write the correct letter next to the occupation.

1. waitress _____

2. waiter _____

3. baker _____

4. cook _____

5. cashier _____

6. dishwasher _____

B. Write the missing words.

1.

Tony Vargas is a _____ .

It's _____ and

_____ at work.

2.

Ms. Turner is a _____ .

It's _____ and

_____ at work.

3.

Boris and Mario are _____ .

It's _____ and

_____ at work.

4.

Write about you.

I'm a _____ .

It's _____ and

_____ at school.

C. Look at the pictures. Change the sentences.

1. He's a doctor.

They're doctors.

2. She's a cook.

_____

3. She's a teacher.

_____

4. He's a nurse.

_____

5. She's a student.

_____

6. He's a teacher.

_____

D. Look at the pictures. Answer the questions.

1. Is Joe a barber?

   Yes, he's a barber.

2. Is Norma a teacher?

   _____

3. Is Fruzan a student?

   _____

4. Are Jane and Joe doctors?

   _____

5. Are Bob and Tom waiters?

   _____

6. Are they students?

   _____

What's His Name?

Objective: In this lesson you will learn to ask about someone's name.

✔ Review: Occupations

Ask four classmates about their jobs.

Examples: S1: Are you a waiter?
S2: Yes, I am.
S1: Are you a salesclerk?
S3: No, I'm not. I'm a cook.

Write their names and their answers in the spaces.

Name	Occupation	Yes	No	Real Occupation
_____	waiter	____	____	_____
_____	salesclerk	____	____	_____
_____	homemaker	____	____	_____
_____	baker	____	____	_____

Something New: His and Her
Listen and Look

His name's Ben Lee.

Her name's Sue Duran.

☛ Practice Activity: My name's Sue

Practice in groups.

My name's _____ .   His name's _____ .

Your name's _____ .   Her name's _____ .

Let's Talk: What's Her Name?

May and Sara are talking about a new student.

May: She's very beautiful.
      Is she a new student?
Sara: Yes, she is. She's my friend.
May: What's her name?
Sara: (Her name's) Sue Duran.

☛ **Practice: "What's his name?"**

1. S1: He's good–looking.
   Is he a new student?
   S2: Yes, he is.
   S1: What's his name?
   S2: His name's Ben Lee.

2. S1: She's good–looking.
   Is she your friend?
   S2: Yes, she is.
   S1: What's her name?
   S2: Her name's Sue Duran.

★ **Something Extra:** Pronunciation

His	**He's**
/ɪ/	/iy/
His name's Ben Lee.	He's a waiter.

| His name's Joe Martin. | He's a salesclerk. |

☞ Practice Activity: I think it's his pen

1. Form a group of students.
2. Each student put an object (a pencil, pen, dictionary, etc.) on the table.
3. Practice asking about the objects.

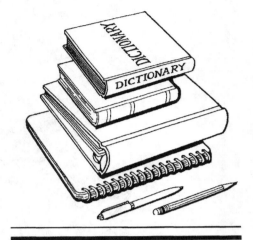

   - Pick up one object.
   - Ask another student about the object.

   Example: S1: Excuse me. Is this your pen?

   S2: No, it isn't. Maybe it's his pen.
   (S2 points to another student.)

   S1: Excuse me. Is this your pen?

   S3: No, it isn't. Maybe it's her pen.

   - Continue to ask until you find the owner.

★ Something Extra: Writing

Write about yourself.

_____ name is _____ . _____

address is _____ .

I am a _____ .

Write about a classmate.

_____ name is _____ . _____

address is _____ .

_____ is a _____ .

Reading: Two Students

Her name is Lucy Moreno. She's a secretary. His name is Tom Morita. He's a baker. They are students, too. It's 7 o'clock in the evening. They are in class now.

✎ Writing

1. What's her name?

   _____ .

2. Is she a nurse?

   _____ .

3. What's his name?

   _____ .

4. Is he a baker?

   _____ .

5. Is he a student, too?

   _____ .

6. What time is it?

   _____ .

7. Are they in class now?

   _____ .

Lesson 9 Activity Pages

A. *Look at the picture and write the correct word.*

His	students	They	Her	waiter	are

This is Jim Sanchez. He is a _____ . _____ friend is

a waitress. _____ name is Martha Widawsky. Jim and Martha are restaurant

workers in the daytime. _____ are students at night. They are good workers,

good _____ and good friends.

B. Write the words in the boxes. Listen and circle the words you hear. Three circles in a row = BINGO!!

<u>**Word List**</u>

waiter

homemaker

doctor

nurse

salesclerk

cook

student

secretary

teacher

Unit Three **Evaluation**

I. Listening Comprehension

Listen to the teacher. Circle the correct answer, A or B.

1.

A   B

2.

A   B

3.

A   B

4.

A   B

5.

A   B

6.

A. Yes, he is.   B. No, he isn't.

7.

A. Yes, he is.   B. Yes, she is.

8.

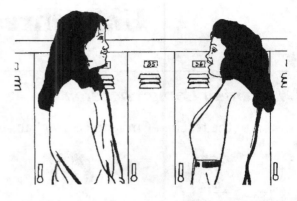

A. Yes, we are.   B. Yes, they are.

9.

A. Yes, they are.   B. No, they aren't.

10.

A. Yes, he is.   B. Yes, they are.

II. Reading

Circle the correct answer.

1. Is he a _____ ?

   doctor   name   lawyers

2. _____ , he is.

   What   No   Yes

3. He's a _____ .

   name   sales   teacher

4. _____ a baker.

   What   She's   His

5. What's her _____ ?

   homemaker   name   nurse

6. _____ dentists.

   He's   She's   They're

III. Writing

Choose the correct word and write it on the line.

1. Is he a barber?

   No, he _____ .

2. Are they teachers?

   Yes, they _____ .

3. Are you students?

   Yes, _____ are.

are
nurses
He's
Her
His
I
isn't
She's
waiter
we

4. They're _____ .

5. _____ name's June Baker.

6. _____ name's Tho Nguyen.

Notes

Unit Four

Nickels and Dimes

How Much Is It?

Objectives: In this lesson you will learn the names of U.S. coins. You will also learn some food items and talk about the price of these items.

✔ Review: Names and Occupations

Look at the pictures. Practice telling names and jobs.

  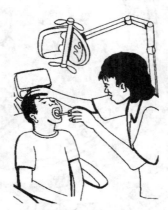 

| Olga Landau | Ricardo Rossini | Haidy Diaz | Tae Wu |

Something New: U.S. Coins
Listen and Look

| a penny | a nickel | a dime | a quarter | a half–dollar |
| 1 cent | 5 cents | 10 cents | 25 cents | 50 cents |

☛ **Practice: "What's this?"**

1. S1: What's this?
   S2: It's a penny.

2. S1: What's this?
   S2: It's a quarter.

3. S1: How much is a nickel?
   S2: It's 5 cents.

4. S1: How much is a dime?
   S2: It's 10 cents.

Something New: Food Items

Listen and Look

a doughnut
40 cents

a muffin
75 cents

a small cup of coffee
35 cents

a medium cup of coffee
50 cents

a large cup of coffee
65 cents

a bottle of apple juice
65 cents

a bottle of orange juice
80 cents

Soft Drinks—60 cents

A can of Cal–Cola

A can of Lemon–Up

Let's Talk: How Much Is It?

It's break time at the adult school. The food truck is at the school.

Ruben: Is this a large cup of coffee?

Cashier: No, it's a medium.

Ruben: How much is it?

Cashier: It's 50 cents.

☛ **Practice: "It's a bottle of orange juice"**

1. S1: What's this?
   S2: It's a bottle of orange juice.

2. S1: How much is this can of Cal–Cola?
   S2: It's 60 cents.

3. S1: Is this a small (cup)?
   S2: No, it isn't. It's a medium (cup of coffee).

4. S1: What size is this cup?
   S2: It's a small (size).

5. S1: How much is a cup of coffee?
   S2: What size?
   S1: A large (size).
   S2: It's 65 cents.

■ Interaction: At the Food Truck

Practice buying food items from the truck.
Ask and answer questions.

Is this a - - - - - - - - - - - - - - - - - ?

What's - - - - - - - - - - - - - - - - - - - ?

What size - - - - - - - - - - - - - - - - ?

How much - - - - - - - - - - - - - - - ?

Reading: The Lunch Truck

It's break time at work. Mr. Benson's Rolling Lunch Truck is in the parking lot. Joe and Bill are at the truck. A small cup of coffee is 50 cents. A soft drink is 75 cents. A muffin is 75 cents, too.

Discussion

1. Is the truck at school or at work?
2. Is a small cup of coffee 50 cents?
3. How much is a soft drink?
4. How much is a muffin?

5. What's your favorite food from the truck?
6. How much is it?
7. Is the food at your school cheap or expensive?

✎ **Writing**

1. What's this?

_____.

How much is it?

_____.

2. Is a bottle of juice 50 cents?

_____.

How much is it?

_____.

3. _____?

It's a dime._____

_____?

It's 10 cents. _____

4. Is this a small (cup of coffee)?

_____.

What size is it?

_____.

■ Interaction: How Many Coins Do You Have?

1. Take out the coins from your pocket or purse.

2. Ask: *How many coins are in your pocket/purse?*
     How many pennies, nickels, dimes, quarters?
     How much money is it?

3. Tell the class who has the most pennies:

_____

nickels: _____

dimes: _____

quarters: _____

half–dollars: _____

_____

Lesson 10 Activity Pages

A. Listen. Write the correct letter.

1.  *d*   a.

2.  _____   b.

3.  _____   c.

4.  _____   d.

5.  _____   e.

B. Write the question.

Write: "What's this?" or "How much is this?" or "What size is this?"

1. _____ *What's this* _____ ?   It's a muffin.

2. _____ ?   It's 40 cents.

3. _____ ?   It's a medium.

4. _____ ?   It's a soft drink.

5. _____ ?   It's 80 cents.

6. _____ ?   It's a large.

7. _____ ?   It's tea.

8. _____ ?   It's orange juice.
   _____ ?   It's a small.
   _____ ?   It's 50 cents.

How Much Is That Binder?

Objectives: In this lesson you will learn about paper money (bills) and ask and answer questions about items in a student store.

✔ **Review:** Names of Coins and Their Values

Something New: U.S. Money—Bills and Coins

Listen and Look

a 1–dollar bill (a dollar bill)

a 5–dollar bill

a 10–dollar bill

a 20–dollar bill

1 dollar is 100 cents.

1 dollar

1 dollar

1 dollar

How many coins are there?

How much is it?

Something New: It's $1.75

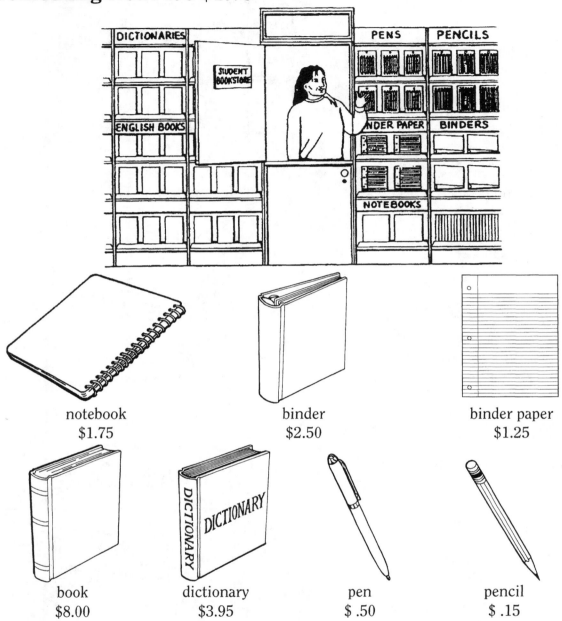

notebook
$1.75

binder
$2.50

binder paper
$1.25

book
$8.00

dictionary
$3.95

pen
$ .50

pencil
$ .15

- This notebook is 1 dollar and 75 cents. It's one seventy–five. It's cheap.
- That binder is 2 dollars and 50 cents. It's two fifty. It's expensive.
- Paper for the binder is 1 dollar and 25 cents. It's one twenty–five. It's expensive.
- This book for the English class is 8 dollars.
- That dictionary is 3 dollars and 95 cents. It's three ninety–five.
- This pen is 50 cents. That pencil is 15 cents.

☞ **Practice: "It's a binder"**

1. S1: What's this?
   S2: It's a notebook.

2. S1: What's that?
   S2: It's a binder.

3. S1: How much is the book
   for the English class?
   S2: It's 8 dollars.

4. S1: How much is the dictionary?
   S2: It's 3 dollars and 95 cents.
   (It's three ninety–five.)

Let's Talk: How Much Is That Binder?

This is the first day of school for Maria.

Clerk: May I help you?

Maria: Yes, please. How much
is that binder?

Clerk: It's two fifty, and the
paper is one twenty–five.

Maria: Oh, my! It's expensive!

Clerk: This notebook is only
one seventy–five.

☛ Practice: "It's three ninety–five"

1. S1: How much is that dictionary?
   S2: It's three ninety–five.
   S1: Oh, good! It's cheap!

2. S1: How much is this book?
   S2: It's eight fifty.
   S1: Oh, my! It's expensive!

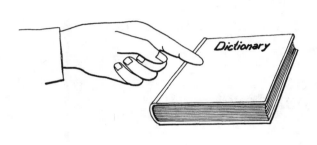

3. S1: What's that?
   S2: It's a dictionary.
   S1: How much is it?
   S2: It's $3.95.

4. S1: Is this book expensive?
   S2: Well, it's $8.50.
   S1: Oh! That's expensive!

☛ Practice Activity: Prices

Listen and write the price of the items you hear.

1. book   _$6.50_

2. pencil   _____

3. notebook   _____

4. dictionary   _____

5. binder   _____

6. pen   _____

Reading: The Student Bookstore

The student bookstore is a busy place. There are new students at the bookstore every night. They ask questions about the books, notebooks, pens, and pencils. Some items are expensive and some items are cheap.

Discussion

1. Is there a bookstore at your school?
2. What can you buy at the bookstore?
3. Are the items cheap or expensive?
4. How much is the book for this class?
5. How much are other items in the store?

Writing: Westside Adult School Bookstore

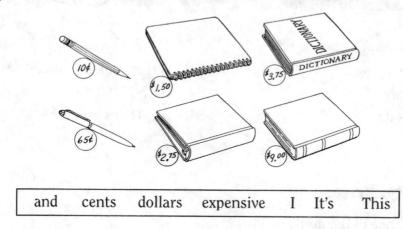

and	cents	dollars	expensive	I	It's	This

This is my first day at Westside Adult School. _____ am at the student bookstore.

_____ is the book for my class. It is nine _____. It's

expensive. This binder is 2 dollars _____ 75 cents. That dictionary is 3

dollars and 75 _____ . It isn't _____ .

Lesson 11 Activity Pages

A. Read the sentence and circle the correct letter.

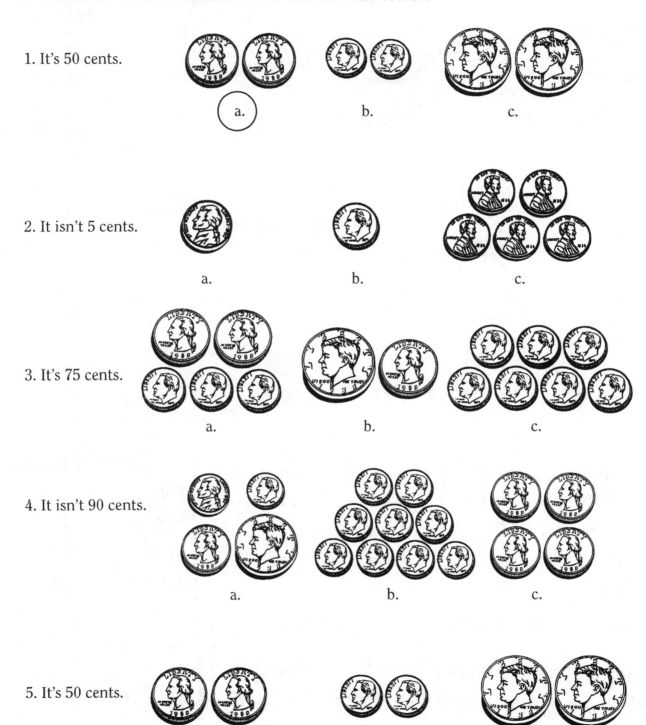

1. It's 50 cents.
   a.   b.   c.

2. It isn't 5 cents.
   a.   b.   c.

3. It's 75 cents.
   a.   b.   c.

4. It isn't 90 cents.
   a.   b.   c.

5. It's 50 cents.
   a.   b.   c.

B. Work with a partner. Ask "How much is a _____?"

1.

2.

3.

4.

5.

6.

7.

C. Listen and write the prices on the receipts.

1.

BOOKSTORE	
BINDER........	$ 2.50
PAPER........	$.
PEN..........	$.
PENCIL.......	$ .15
DICTIONARY...	$ 3.95
TOTAL........	$ 9.60

2.

BOOKSTORE	
TEXTBOOK.....	$ 8.00
NOTEBOOK.....	$.
PENCIL.......	$.
PENCIL.......	$.
DICTIONARY...	$.
TOTAL........	$ 14.25

3.

BOOKSTORE	
PEN..........	$.
PEN..........	$.
BINDER.......	$.
BINDER.......	$.
TEXTBOOK.....	$.
DICTIONARY...	$.
TOTAL........	$.

D. Circle the correct change.

1.

a. $ .50   (b.) $ .25   c. $2.50

2.

a. $1.50   b. $12.50   c. $1.25

3.

a. $4.01   b. $6.01   c. $6.99

4.

a. $ .50   b. $50.00   c. $5.00

For Here or To Go?

Objective: In this lesson you will learn to order food from a fast–food restaurant.

✔ **Review:** Money

★ ★ ★ H E L P   W A N T E D ★ ★ ★

Restaurant Workers	Dishwashers —— $4.25/hr. Waiters —— $8.75/hr. Cooks —— $7.50/hr.
Hospital Workers	Nurses —— $11.25/hr. Hospital Clerks —— $ 6.50/hr.
School Workers	School Clerks —— $5.30/hr.

1. Read the newspaper ads. Practice saying the pay for the workers.
2. Practice saying the pay first the long way, then the short way.

   Example: "Dishwashers—4 dollars and 25 cents an hour.
   "Dishwashers—four twenty–five an hour."

Something New: Fast Food
Listen and Look

a hamburger — a hamburger with cheese (a cheeseburger) — a hot dog

french fries — a carton of milk

☛ Practice Activity: Ordering fast food

This is the menu from MacBurger's, a fast–food restaurant. The menu is on the wall:

Sandwiches		Side Orders		Beverages	
Hamburger	1.50	French Fries		Soft Drinks	
Cheeseburger	1.70	– Small	.59	Cal–Cola & Lemon–Up	
Hot Dog	1.15	– Large	.79	– Small	.70
				– Regular	.85
				– Large	.90
				Coffee	
				– Small	.50
				– Large	.65
				Milk	.50

MacBurger's

Discussion

1. How much is a hamburger? How much is a cheeseburger?
2. How much is a hot dog?
3. What sizes are the french fries? How much is each size?
4. What kinds of soft drinks are there? What sizes are they?
5. What sizes are the cups of coffee? How much is each size?
6. How much is a carton of milk?

Let's Talk: For Here or To Go?

Clerk: May I take your order?

Sara: Yes, please. A cheeseburger, french fries, and a large cola, please.

Clerk: (Is that) For here or to go?

Sara: For here.

☛ Practice: "A hot dog, fries, and a small coffee"

1. S1: May I take your order, please?

   S2: Yes, please. A hot dog, fries, and a small coffee.

2. S1: For here or to go?

   S2: To go.

■ Interaction: At a Fast–Food Restaurant

Practice with a partner. One student is a customer and one student is a clerk.

Customer: Place your order. Say "for here" or "to go."
Pay for your order.

Clerk: Listen to the order. Repeat the order.
Ask the customer, "For here or to go?"
Tell the customer how much the order is.

Reading: The Fast Life

Today, life is fast. Cars are fast. Airplanes are fast. Food is fast, too. There are fast–food restaurants all over the world, too. Burger King™ is popular in England and France. McDonald's™ is very popular in Japan and in Russia, too.

Discussion

1. Are there many fast–food restaurants near your home, school, or work? What are their names?

2. Is it good to have fast–food restaurants?

■ Interaction: May I Take Your Order?

Ask three students for their orders. Write each person's name and order in the box.

	Name	To Eat	To Drink
Example:	Mrs. Baker	Cheeseburger	Large Orange Drink
1.	_____	_____	_____
2.	_____	_____	_____
3.	_____	_____	_____

✎ Writing

am	are	coffee	fries	hamburgers	milk	much	is	regular

I _____ at a fast–food restaurant. This _____ my order for

my family: 3 _____ and a hot dog, 4 french _____ , 2

large cups of _____ , and 2 cartons of _____ . How

_____ is it?

★ **Something Extra:** Pronunciation

Numbers Ending in "–ty"

10 — ten	**50** — fifty	**90** — ninety
20 — twenty	**60** — sixty	**100** — one–hundred (a hundred)
30 — thirty	**70** — seventy	
40 — forty	**80** — eighty	

Numbers Ending in "–teen"

13 — thirteen	**17** — seventeen
14 — fourteen	**18** — eighteen
15 — fifteen	**19** — nineteen
16 — sixteen	

1. Listen to the teacher.
   Repeat the numbers.

2. Close your book.
   Listen to the numbers.
   Show which column you hear, 1 or 2.

Column 1

thirteen

fifteen

sixteen

eighteen

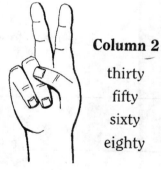

Column 2

thirty

fifty

sixty

eighty

3. Listen to the teacher.
   Write the number you hear.

1. _____
2. _____
3. _____
4. _____
5. _____

6. _____
7. _____
8. _____
9. _____
10. _____

Lesson 12 Activity Page

A. Talk about the picture.

Hamburger	1.50	Soft Drink	Cal-Cola	
Cheeseburger	1.70	Small .70	Reg .85	Large .90
Hot Dog	1.15	Coffee	Small .50	Large .65
Salad	1.95			
French Fries	.59	Milk	.50	
Large	.79			

B. Look at the picture. Read the questions. Circle the answers.

1. Is that a hot dog or a hamburger? (a.) a hamburger   b. a hot dog

2. How much is it?   a. $1.50   b. $1.15

3. What size is his cola?   a. small   b. large

4. Is the milk 50 cents?   a. yes   b. no

C. Look at the picture. Write two questions and answer the questions.

Example: Q. How much is his cola?
A. It's 90 cents.

1. Q. _____ ?

   A. _____ .

2. Q. _____ ?

   A. _____ .

Notes

Unit Four  Evaluation

I. Listening Comprehension

Listen to the teacher. Circle the correct answer, A or B.

1.

A   B

2.

A   B

3.

A. regular   B. 50 cents

4.

A. 80 cents   B. 60 cents

5.

A   B

6.

A. $2.50   B. $1.25

7.

A. a doughnut   B. a muffin

8.

A. a carton   B. 50 cents
   of milk

II. Reading

Circle the correct answer.

1. How _____ is it?

   nickel   much   cents

2. It's 50 _____ .

   cents   dollars   money

3. _____ is a book.

   This   That's   How

4. _____ a hot dog.

   That's   What's   It's

5. What _____ is it?

   much   size   cents

6. It's a _____ of coffee.

   large   size   cup

III. Writing

Write the correct question or answer on the line.

1. What's this?

   _____ .

   How much is it?

   _____ .

2. _____ ?

   It's a pencil.

   _____ ?

   It's 20 cents.

3. How much is it?

   _____ .

4. How much is it?

   _____ .

Unit Five

Days and Dates

Tuesday's My Day Off

Objectives: In this lesson you will learn to talk about the days of the week and days off from work. You will also learn ordinal numbers from 1st to 31st.

✔ Review: Fast Foods

Copy a MacBurger's menu on the chalkboard.

1. Student 1 be a customer. Ask questions and order from the menu.
2. Student 2 be the clerk. Answer the customer's questions and take the order.

Something New: A Calendar
Listen and Look

January

Sunday	Monday	Tuesday	Wednesday	Thursday	Friday	Saturday
					1	2
3	4	5	6	7	8	9
10	11	12	13	14	15	16
17	18	19	20	21	22	23
24 31	25	26	27	28	29	30

Days of the Week:

Sun.—Sunday   Tues.—Tuesday   Fri.—Friday
Mon.—Monday   Wed.—Wednesday   Sat.—Saturday
                 Thurs.—Thursday

☛ **Practice: "What day is it?"**

Sun. (Mon.) Tues. Wed. Thurs. Fri. Sat.   Sun. Mon. Tues. Wed. (Thurs.) Fri. Sat.

1. S1: What day is it?   2. S1: What day is it?
   S2: It's Monday.   S2: It's Thursday.

Sun. Mon. Tues. Wed. Thurs. Fri. (Sat.)   Sun. Mon. (Tues.) Wed. Thurs. Fri. Sat.

3. S1: Is it Saturday or Sunday?   4. S1: Is today Thursday?
   S2: It's - - - - - - - - - - - - - - -.   S2: No, it isn't. It's - - - - - - - - - - - - - - -.

Let's Talk: Tuesday Is My Day Off

It's Monday. The workday is over and Sam and Rosa are leaving for home.

Sam: So long, Rosa. See
you tomorrow.

Rosa: No, tomorrow is
Tuesday. It's my
day off.

Sam: See you on
Wednesday, then.

Rosa: Okay. When is your
day off, Sam?

Sam: It's Thursday.

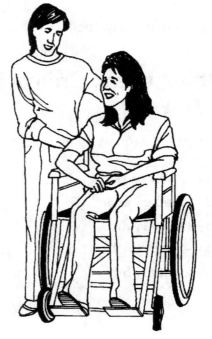

yesterday
today
tomorrow

☛ **Practice: "When is your day off?"**

S1: When is your day off? S2: It's Monday. When's your day off? S3: It's Friday.

☛ **Practice: "See you on Tuesday, then"**

1. S1: When is your day off?
   S2: It's Monday.
   S1: See you on Tuesday, then.

2. S1: When is your day off?
   S2: It's Thursday.
   S1: See you on Friday, then.

★ **Something Extra:** Ordinal Numbers

Listen and Look

Look at the month of January again. Listen to the days of the month.

January 1 —January 1st
January 2 —January 2nd
January 3 —January 3rd
January 4 —January 4th
January 5 —January 5th

January 6 — January 6th
January 7 — January 7th
January 8 — January 8th
January 9 — January 9th
January 10 — January 10th

Jan. 11 — 11th	Jan. 18 — 18th	Jan. 25 — 25th
12 — 12th	19 — 19th	26 — 26th
13 — 13th	20 — 20th	27 — 27th
14 — 14th	21 — 21st	28 — 28th
15 — 15th	22 — 22nd	29 — 29th
16 — 16th	23 — 23rd	30 — 30th
17 — 17th	24 — 24th	31 — 31st

☛ **Practice: "What's the date today?"**

January

10	11	12	13	14	15	16
17	18	19	20	21	22	23

1. S1: What's the date today?
   S2: It's the 15th.

January

17	18	19	20	21	22	23
24/31	25	26	27	28	29	30

2. S1: What's the date today?
   S2: It's the 23rd.

January

					1	2
3	4	5	6	7	8	9

3. S1: What's today's date?
   S2: It's the 2nd.

January

17	18	19	20	21	22	23
24/31	25	26	27	28	29	30

4. S1: Is today the 30th?
   S2: No, it isn't. It's the 31st.

☛ **Practice: "What day is the 20th?"**

Sunday	Monday	Tuesday	Wednesday	Thursday	Friday	Saturday
10	11	12	13	14	15	16
17	18	19	20	21	22	23
24/31	25	26	27	28	29	30

5. S1: What day is the 20th?
   S2: It's - - - - - - - - - - - - - - - - .

6. S1: What day is the 22nd?
   S2: It's - - - - - - - - - - - - - - - - .

■ Interaction: Standing in Line

1. Seven students go to the front of the room and stand in line.
2. Ask questions about the students.

   Example: S1: Who's the *3rd* person in line?

   S2: *Tony.*

3. Give directions. The students in line will follow directions.

   Example: S1: Will the *2nd* and *4th* persons change places?

Reading: Time for School

Today is Monday. It is a school day for Mira. She goes to school four days a week: Monday, Tuesday, Wednesday, and Thursday.

It is time for school. Mira is late. Hurry, Mira.

Discussion

1. What are Mira's school days?
2. Are you early or late for school every day? For work?
3. What is your favorite day of the week?

✍ Writing

1. Write the days of the week.

   _____Sunday_____   _____

   _____   _____

   _____   _____

   _____

2. Write in the missing days.

January

	Mon.			Thurs.		Sat.
					1	2
3	4	5	6	7	8	9

3. Write the answers.

   a. What's the date today?

      _____.

   b. What day is it?

      _____.

   c. What are your days for school?

      _____.

   d. What are your days for work?

      _____.

Lesson 13 Activity Pages

A. Listen and circle the correct days.

1.   Sun.   Mon.   Tues.   Wed.   Thurs.   (Fri.)   Sat.

2.   Sun.   Mon.   Tues.   Wed.   Thurs.   Fri.   Sat.

3.   Sun.   Mon.   Tues.   Wed.   Thurs.   Fri.   Sat.

4.   Sun.   Mon.   Tues.   Wed.   Thurs.   Fri.   Sat.

5.   Sun.   Mon.   Tues.   Wed.   Thurs.   Fri.   Sat.

6.   Sun.   Mon.   Tues.   Wed.   Thurs.   Fri.   Sat.

7.   Sun.   Mon.   Tues.   Wed.   Thurs.   Fri.   Sat.

8.   Sun.   Mon.   Tues.   Wed.   Thurs.   Fri.   Sat.

B. Talk about the picture.

C. Choose the correct word. Fill in the blanks.

1st	2nd	3rd	4th	5th	6th	five	one	Monday

Today is _Monday_____ , the _____ . See the people in line?

They're waiting for the lunch truck. Two women are standing in line. One woman is the

_____ person in line, and one woman is the _____ person in line. The 1st

person in line is holding a _____ dollar bill and the 2nd person in line is holding a

_____ dollar bill.

Lesson 14

When Is Your Birthday?

Objectives: In this lesson you will learn to use the calendar to talk about dates. You will also talk about birthdays.

✔ Review: Days of the Week and Ordinal Numbers

Days of the Week

Say the days of the week. Write them on the chalkboard.

Write the abbreviations for the days.

Ordinal Numbers

Ask questions: Who's the 1st person in your row? The 2nd? The 3rd? Etc.

Who's the 1st person in the 1st row? Who's the 3rd person in the 1st row? Etc.

Something New: The Months of the Year

Listen and Look

19_ _

2011

JANUARY	FEBRUARY	MARCH	APRIL	MAY	JUNE
1 2	1 2 3 4 5 6	1 2 3 4 5 6	1 2 3	1	1 2 3 4 5
3 4 5 6 7 8 9	7 8 9 10 11 12 13	7 8 9 10 11 12 13	4 5 6 7 8 9 10	2 3 4 5 6 7 8	6 7 8 9 10 11 12
10 11 12 13 14 15 16	14 15 16 17 18 19 20	14 15 16 17 18 19 20	11 12 13 14 15 16 17	9 10 11 12 13 14 15	13 14 15 16 17 18 19
17 18 19 20 21 22 23	21 22 23 24 25 26 27	21 22 23 24 25 26 27	18 19 20 21 22 23 24	16 17 18 19 20 21 22	20 21 22 23 24 25 26
24 25 26 27 28 29 30	28	28 29 30 31	25 26 27 28 29 30	23 24 25 26 27 28 29	27 28 29 30
31				30 31	

JULY	AUGUST	SEPTEMBER	OCTOBER	NOVEMBER	DECEMBER
1 2 3	1 2 3 4 5 6 7	1 2 3 4	1 2	1 2 3 4 5 6	1 2 3 4
4 5 6 7 8 9 10	8 9 10 11 12 13 14	5 6 7 8 9 10 11	3 4 5 6 7 8 9	7 8 9 10 11 12 13	5 6 7 8 9 10 11
11 12 13 14 15 16 17	15 16 17 18 19 20 21	12 13 14 15 16 17 18	10 11 12 13 14 15 16	14 15 16 17 18 19 20	12 13 14 15 16 17 18
18 19 20 21 22 23 24	22 23 24 25 26 27 28	19 20 21 22 23 24 25	17 18 19 20 21 22 23	21 22 23 24 25 26 27	19 20 21 22 23 24 25
25 26 27 28 29 30 31	29 30 31	26 27 28 29 30	24 25 26 27 28 29 30	28 29 30	26 27 28 29 30 31
			31		

Delta's Apple Pie, Book 1A

☛ Practice: "What's the 3rd month of the year?"

1. S1: What's the 3rd month of the year?

   S2: It's March.

2. S1: What's the 8th month of the year?

   S2: It's August.

3. S1: What's the 10th month of the year?

   S2: It's October.

4. S1: What's the 5th month of the year?

   S2: It's May.

☛ Practice: "What's the date?"

1. S1: What's the date?

   S2: It's April 4th.

2. S1: What's the date?

   S2: It's August 23rd.

3. S1: What's today's date?

   S2: It's - - - - - - - - - - - - - - .

4. S1: Is today the 20th?

   S2: No, it isn't. It's the - - - - - - - - - .

Let's Talk: When Is Your Birthday?

May: When is your birthday, Sue?

Sue: It's on February 14th.

May: Is that Valentine's Day?

Sue: Yes, it is. It's my favorite day of the year!

☛ **Practice: "It's on May 1st"**

May

Sunday	Monday	Tuesday	Wednesday	Thursday	Friday	Saturday
						1
2	3	4	5	6	7	8
9	10	11	12	13	14	15

October

Sunday	Monday	Tuesday	Wednesday	Thursday	Friday	Saturday
10	11	12	13	14	15	16
17	18	19	20	21	22	23
24 31	25	26	27	28	29	30

1. S1: When is Mario's birthday?
   S2: It's on May 1st.

2. S1: When is her birthday?
   S2: It's on October 20th.

■ **Interaction:** What's Your Birthday Month?

1. Make a sign for each month.
2. Put the signs around the room.
3. Go to the sign for your birthday month.
4. Talk to the other students with the same birthday month.

   Example: S1: Is your birthday in June, too?

   S2: Yes, it is.

   S1: When is your birthday?

   S2: It's on the 20th.

   S1: My birthday is on the 6th.

5. Stand in line in order of your birthdates.

Reading: Happy Birthday, Mr. Wong

Sue: Hello, Mr. Wong. How are you?

Mr. Wong: Fine, thank you. It's my birthday today.

Sue: How old are you now?

Mr. Wong: I'm 82 years old.

Sue: Happy birthday, Mr. Wong.

Discussion

1. How old is Mr. Wong today?
2. When is your birthday?
3. What do you like to do on your birthday?

✍ Writing

1. Complete the sentences.

   a. August is the _____ month of the year.

   b. October is the _____ month of the year.

   c. _____ is the 11th month of the year.

   d. _____ is the 3rd month of the year.

2. Write the questions or answers.

   a. When is Mr. Wong's birthday? _____ .

   b. When is your birthday? _____ .

   c. _____ ?

   It's February 14th.

★ Something Extra: Birthdays of Presidents

Abraham Lincoln and George Washington are two famous presidents of the United States of America.

President Lincoln's birthday
is on February 12th.

President Washington's birthday
is on February 22nd.

☞ Practice: "Yes, they are"

February

Sunday	Monday	Tuesday	Wednesday	Thursday	Friday	Saturday
	1	2	3	4	5	6
7	8	9	10	11	12	13
14	15	16	17	18	19	20
21	22	23	24	25	26	27
28						

1. S1: Are the birthdays of Lincoln
   and Washington in February?
   S2: Yes, they are.

2. S1: When is Lincoln's birthday?
   S2: It's on the - - - - - - - - .

3. S1: When is Washington's birthday?
   S2: It's on the - - - - - - - - .

4. S1: When is Valentine's Day?
   S2: It's on the - - - - - - - - .

Lesson 14 Activity Pages

A. Look at the calendar. Listen and circle the dates you hear.

February

Sunday	Monday	Tuesday	Wednesday	Thursday	Friday	Saturday
1	2	3	4	5	6	
7	8	9	10	11		13
♥	15	16	17	18	19	20
21		23	24	25	26	27
28	29					

B. Look at the calendar and write the days and ordinal numbers.

On this calendar Lincoln's birthday is Friday, February _____ .

Valentine's Day is _____ , February _____ . Washington's

birthday is _____ February _____ . There's an extra day in

February on this calendar. It's _____ , February _____ .

C. Write the months next to the dates.

1/3	_January_	3	7/4	_____	4, 1776
5/14	_____	14	10/31	_____	31
12/25	_____	25	6/14	_____	14
2/12	_____	12	11/20	_____	20

D. Listen and do it.

1.

2.

3.

4.

5.

6.

E. Look at the picture and follow the directions.

1. Circle the 31st on the calendar.

2. Write the month on the calendar. (It's the 7th month.)

3. Write "Apple Juice" on the bottle.

4. Draw a party hat on the 3rd person.

5. Draw 9 presents on the table.

6. Write the name "JANE" on the cake.

7. Put some candles on the cake.

Where Are You From?

Objectives: In this lesson you will learn to ask and answer questions about your native country, and talk about cities, states, and countries.

✔ Review: When Is Your Birthday?

Students will write their birthdays on the chalkboard. Read the dates.

Something New: The Map of the World
Listen and Look

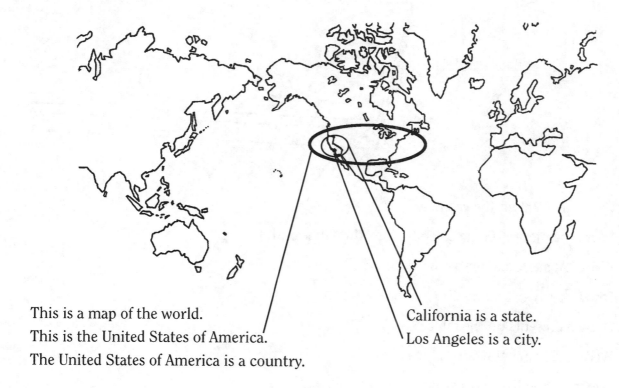

This is a map of the world.

This is the United States of America.

The United States of America is a country.

California is a state.

Los Angeles is a city.

☛ **Practice Activity: My native country**

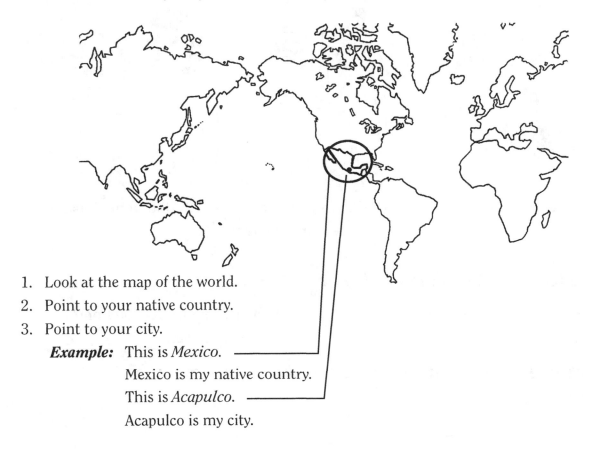

1. Look at the map of the world.
2. Point to your native country.
3. Point to your city.

    Example: This is *Mexico.*

                 Mexico is my native country.

                 This is *Acapulco.*

                 Acapulco is my city.

Let's Talk: Where Are You From?

It's break time and the students are talking in the hall.

    Tony: Sue, this is a new
              student, Miguel.

    Sue: Nice to meet you,
            Miguel. Where are
            you from?

Miguel: I'm from Peru.

    Sue: I'm from Peru, too.
            What city are you
            from?

Miguel: Lima.

    Sue: I'm from Lima, too!
            I'm really happy to
            meet you.

☛ **Practice: "Where are you from?"**

S1: Where are you from?

S2: I'm from Korea.
Where are you from?

S3: I'm from China.

☛ **Practice: "What city are you from?"**

1. S1: What city are you from?
   S2: I'm from Managua.

2. S1: What country are you from?
   S2: I'm from Vietnam.

★ **Something Extra:** The United States of America

Listen and Look

The United States of America is a country.

California is a state.

Los Angeles is a city.

New York is a state.

New York City is a city.

Texas is a state.

Dallas is a city.

Illinois is a state.

Chicago is a city.

☞ **Practice: "What's your state?"**

Los Angeles

1. S1: What's your state?
   S2: It's New York.

2. S1: What's your city?
   S2: It's Los Angeles.

3. S1: Is Dallas a city or a state?
   S2: It's a city.

4. S1: Is Chicago a state?
   S2: No, it isn't. It's a city.

■ Interaction: Where Are You From?

1. Look at a large map of the world or the map on page 128.
2. Ask the students in your group: Where are you from?
3. Point to a country on the map. Ask the students in your group: What country is this?

Reading: We Are the World

The students in our class are from many countries. Mario is from Mexico. Sonia is from Nicaragua and Adolfo from Guatemala. Korea is Sook's native country. Tranh comes from Vietnam. Boris is a new student from Russia.

We are one big family.

Discussion

1. Where are you from?
2. People come to the United States for many reasons. Why are you here? To study English? To be with your family? To get a better job?

✍ **Writing**

Complete the questions and answers:

1. Where are the students from?

   _____ .

2. _____ ?

   He's from Russia.

3. What is Sook's native country?

   _____ .

4. What country are you from?

   _____ .

Lesson 15 Activity Pages

A. Read the questions. Write your answers. Then ask your partner the questions.

1. What's your first name?

2. Where are you from?

3. When's your birthday?

4. What days are you in school?

B. Ask four friends for the information on the grid. Write the answers on the grid.

Name	Country	Birthday
Ben Lee	China	September 12

C. BINGO: *Read the directions and play.*

1. Write the dates you hear in the squares.

2. Listen to your teacher and circle the dates you hear.

3. Look for 4 circles in a row and you have BINGO!!

Unit Five Evaluation

I. Listening Comprehension

Listen to the teacher. Circle the correct answer, A or B.

1.

A   B

2.

A   B

A   B

3.

A   B

4.

Illinois   Chicago

A   B

5.

Texas   Mexico

A   B

6.

May
1   May
4

A   B

7.

January   February

A.   B

8.

Sun. Mon. Tues. Wed. Thurs. Fri. Sat.

A. No, it isn't.
B. No, he isn't.

II. Reading

Circle the correct answer.

1. Where _____ you from?

        is   are   am

2. What's the _____ today?

        week   time   date

3. Los Angeles is a _____.

       country   state   city

4. May is the _____ month of the year.

       5th   6th   7th

III. Writing

Choose the correct word and write it on the line.

_____ is Wednesday, May 21st. It's Jaime's

_____. Jaime is from _____.

His _____ is Dallas now.

city
Lima
birthday
It's
Today
country

Write in the days of the week.

1. Sunday

2. _____

3. _____

4. Wednesday

5. _____

6. Friday

7. _____

Unit Six

Of Cabbages and Cakes

It's a Fruit Salad

Objectives: In this lesson you will learn the names of some fruits. You will also talk about how to make a fruit salad.

✔ Review: Introduce a Friend

1. Write your name, native country, and occupation on a card.
2. Give your card to another student. The student will introduce you to the class using the information on the card.

Something New: Names of Fruit

an apple

an orange

a banana

a pear

a watermelon

a lemon

a grapefruit

a fruit salad

a pineapple

☛ **Practice: "It's an apple"**

1. S1: What's this?
   S2: It's an apple.

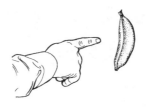

2. S1: What's that?
   S2: It's a banana.

3. S1: What's this?
   S2: It's a pineapple.

4. S1: What's that?
   S2: It's a watermelon.

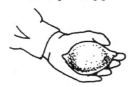

5. S1: Is this a lemon?
   S2: Yes, it is.

6. S1: Is that a pear?
   S2: Yes, it is.

7. S1: Is this an apple?
   S2: No, it isn't. It's an orange.

8. S1: Is that an orange?
   S2: Yes, it is.

Let's Talk: Is This a Fruit Salad?

Sue is at the market. She is in the deli section. She is looking at the salads.

Sue: Is this a fruit salad?

Clerk: Yes, it is.

Sue: How much is it?

Clerk: It's $2.50.

Sue: What's that?

Clerk: It's an orange and grapefruit salad. It's the same price, $2.50.

☛ **Practice: "It's the same price"**

1. S1: How much is this salad?
   S2: It's $2.49.
   S1: How much is that salad?
   S2: It's the same price.

2. S1: Is that salad 75 cents?
   S2: Yes, it is.
   S1: How much is this salad?
   S2: It's the same price.

Something New: Making a Fruit Salad

Let's make a fruit salad. Follow the directions below.

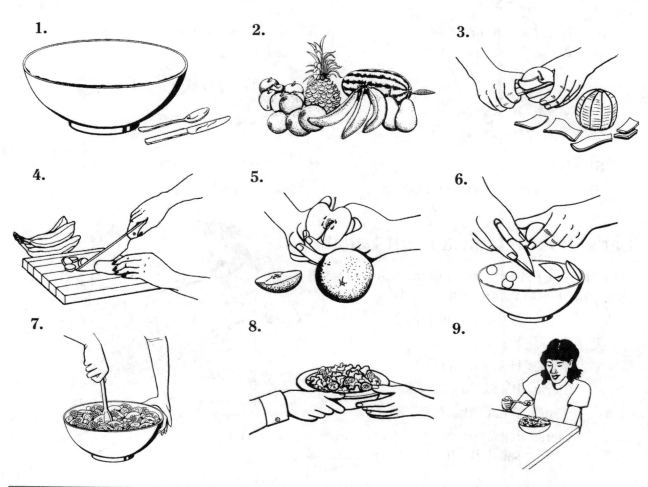

Delta's Apple Pie, Book 1A

☛ Practice: "Cut up the fruit"

Circle the correct answer.

Cut up	the apple	the salad	the bowl
Peel	the salad	the bowl	the orange
Stir	the fruit	the spoon	the knife
Slice	the knife	the bowl	the banana

☛ Practice: "What's first?"

Number the sentences in order.

___7___ Stir the fruit.

___5___ Cut up the apple and orange.

___3___ Peel the banana, apple, and orange.

___8___ Serve the salad.

___1___ Get a bowl, knife, and spoon.

___6___ Put the fruit in the bowl.

___2___ Get the fruit.

___4___ Slice the banana.

___9___ Eat the fruit salad.

Oh, it's delicious!

■ Interaction: How to Make a Fruit Salad

Tell your partner how to make fruit salad.
You can say *First...*, *Then...*, *Next...*, etc.
Your partner will do the actions you say.

spoon

☛ Practice Activity: Giving directions

Write the directions for making fruit salad. Use the words in the boxes.

Get	Cut up		banana	apple
Stir	Eat		fruit	salad
Serve	Slice		bowl	knife
Put	Peel		orange	spoon

1. _Get a bowl fruit knife spoon_____

2. _Peel ~~Put~~ orange_____

3. _____

4. _____

5. _____

6. _____

7. _____

8. _____

9. _____

Reading: At the Cafeteria

I eat lunch at work every day. I like the fruit in the cafeteria. An orange is 75 cents. An apple is the same price, but a banana is 50 cents. The fruit salad is $2.25. Lemon jello is 75 cents.

Handwritten notes in margin: $5, 5¢ same, $.05, $75, 75¢, $.75

✍ Writing

1. How much is lemon jello?

   75 cents .

2. Is a fruit salad 75 cents?

   _No, it is $2.25._ .

3. How much is the fruit salad?

   _$ 2.25_ .

4. Are an apple and an orange the same price?

   Yes, it is $.75 .

5. Is a banana the same price as the apple?

   _NO_ .

6. How much is the banana?

   _it $0.50_ .

Lesson 16 Activity Pages

A. Listen and draw what you hear.

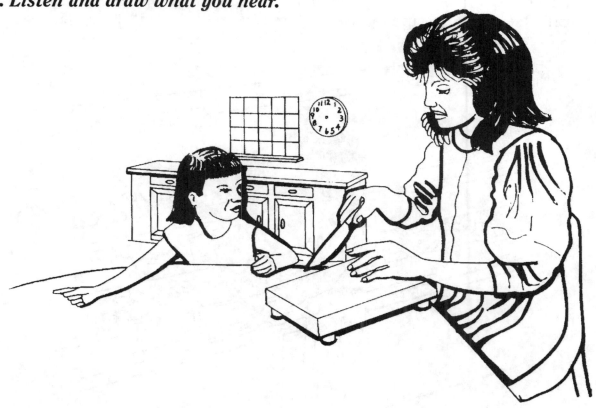

B. Look at the picture. Write the missing words.

you	banana	This	that	bowl

Ann: Give me that ___*bowl*___, please.

Mary: ___*that*___ bowl?

Ann: Yes, thank ___*you*___.

Mary: Peel ___*this*___ banana for me.

Ann: That ___*bowl*___?

Mary: Yes, thanks.

C. Match the sentence to the picture.

Draw a line to the correct picture.

1. That's a banana.

2. This is an orange.

3. This is a banana.

4. That's a grapefruit.

5. That's a lemon.

6. This is a pear.

7. This is an apple.

8. That's a pear.

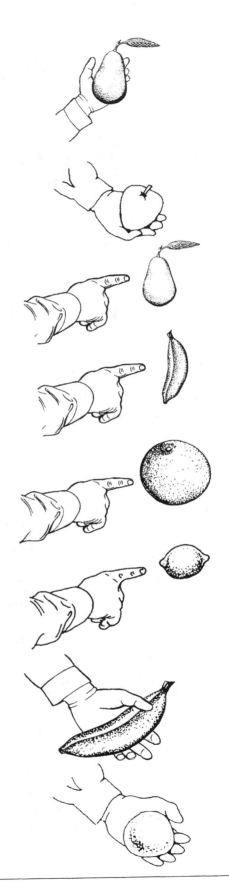

Rosa Buys Vegetables

Objectives: In this lesson you will learn the names of vegetables and ask and answer questions about how much they cost. You will also give and follow directions.

✔ Review: A Fruit Salad

This is a fruit bowl.

Draw one fruit bowl on a piece of paper.

Each student draw a different fruit in the bowl.

Talk about the fruit with your group.

Something New: Vegetables
Listen and Look

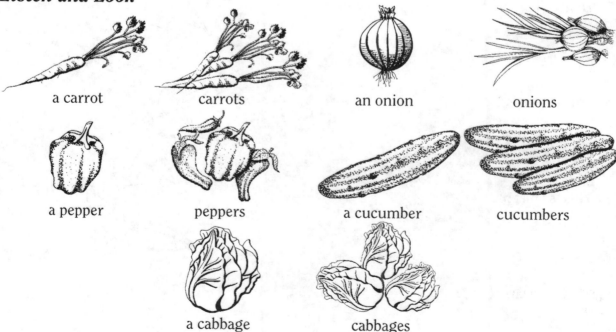

a carrot　　　carrots　　　an onion　　　onions

a pepper　　　peppers　　　a cucumber　　　cucumbers

a cabbage　　　cabbages

☞ **Practice: "Are these onions?"**

1. S1: What are these?
   S2: They're cabbages.

2. S1: What are those?
   S2: They're carrots.

3. S1: Are these onions?
   S2: No, they aren't.
   S1: What are they?
   S2: They're peppers.

4. S1: Are those cucumbers?
   S2: No, they aren't.
   S1: What are they?
   S2: They're cabbages.

Let's Talk: Rosa Buys Vegetables

Rosa is buying vegetables at the produce market.

Rosa: How much are those cucumbers?

Mark: Those (cucumbers) are 75 cents each.
   Those small cucumbers are
   85 cents a pound.

Rosa: Are they for salad, too?

Mark: No, they're for pickles.

☛ **Practice: "They're 60 cents each"**

1. S1: How much are the peppers?
   S2: They're 60 cents each.

2. S1: How much are the onions?
   S2: They're 50 cents a pound.

3. S1: Are carrots 75 cents a bunch?
   S2: Yes, they are.

4. S1: Are bananas 30 cents each
      or 30 cents a pound?
   S2: They're 30 cents a pound.

Reading: An Outdoor Market

Sara and Tomas go to the outdoor market every Friday morning. Everything is cheap there. The carrots are 55 cents a bunch. The cucumbers are 39 cents each. The outdoor market is a good place for fresh vegetables.

Yes or No

1. Carrots are 55 cents a bunch.   yes   no
2. Sara and Tomas like to buy fresh vegetables.   yes   no
3. Cucumbers are 39 cents a pound.   yes   no
4. Vegetables are expensive at the outdoor market.   yes   no

Discussion

1. Is there an outdoor market near your home?
2. Where do you buy your vegetables?
3. Let's make a salad. What vegetables do you want?

✍ Writing

1. Sara: What are those?
   Mark: ___peppers___ .
   Sara: How much are they?
   Mark: ___$0.50___ .

2. Sara: What are these?
   Mark: ___cucumbers___ .
   Sara: How much are they?
   Mark: ___$0.39___ .

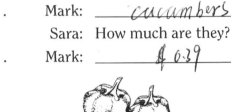

3. Sara: ___What___ are these?
   Mark: They're oranges.
   Sara: ___How much are they___ ?
   Mark: They're 59 cents a pound.

4. Sara: How much are the peppers?
   Mark: ___They're $0.60___ .
   Sara: Are the carrots 79 cents a bunch?
   Mark: ___No, it is $89¢ a bunch___

★ Something Extra: Pronunciation

Listen to the plural sounds of these words.

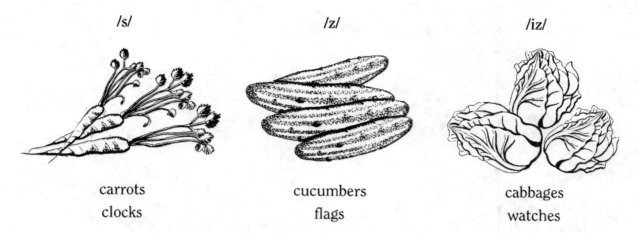

/s/	/z/	/iz/
carrots	cucumbers	cabbages
clocks	flags	watches

Listen to the word. Write the plural sound.

1. books _____s_____
2. pencils _____z_____
3. cabbages _____iz_____
4. bananas _____s_____
5. dentists _____s_____

6. apples _____
7. oranges _____
8. desks _____
9. vegetables _____
10. lemons _____

■ Interaction: A Market

1. Use pictures to set up a market in the classroom.
2. One student be a clerk and one student be a customer. Ask and answer questions about the vegetables.

Lesson 17 Activity Pages

A. Listen and label the vegetables.

CARROTS

B. Look at the answer and write the question. Use "these" or "those."

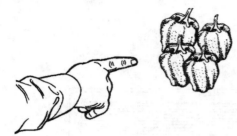 

1. __Are those Peppeves__ ?
   Yes, they are.

2. __thse are apple__ ?
   No, they aren't.

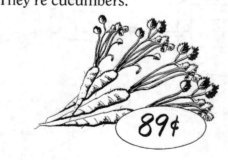 

3. _____ ?
   They're cucumbers.

4. _____ ?
   They're cabbages.

89¢

98¢

5. _____ ?
   They're 89¢.

6. _____ ?
   They're 98¢.

79¢

ONIONS 79¢ LB. POTATOES 49¢ LB.

7. _____ ?
   Yes, they are.

8. _____ ?
   No, they aren't.

C. Look at the vegetable bins. Read and follow the directions.

1. Draw carrots in this bin.

2. Draw cabbages in that bin.

3. Write the name of the vegetable on this bin.

4. Write the price of the vegetable on that bin.

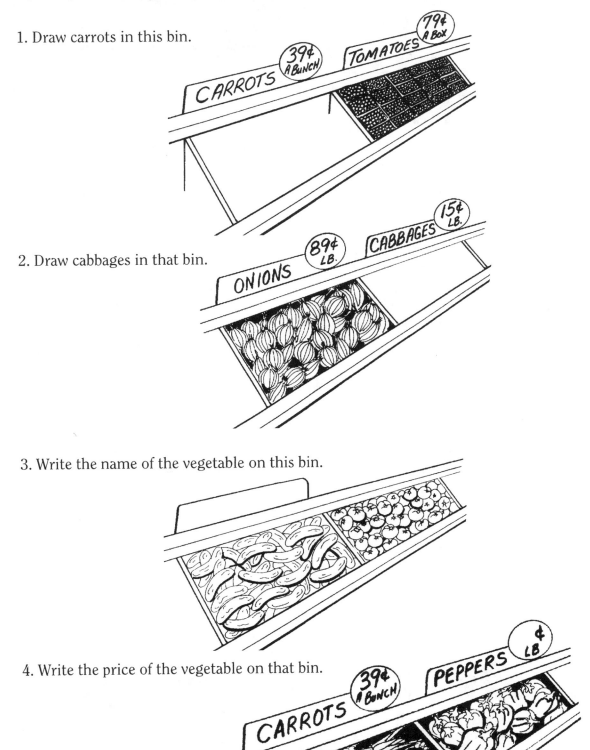

The Bakery

Objectives: In this lesson you will learn some names of bakery items and how to order in a bakery.

✔ Review: Fill the Grocery Bag

Choose fruits and vegetables to put into the grocery bag.

Example:

S1:   One cucumber

S2:   One cucumber, two cabbages

S3:   One cucumber, two cabbages, three carrots

S4:   One cucumber, two cabbages, three carrots, four oranges

Something New: Bakery Items

Listen and Look

a cake

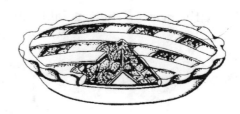

a pie

a loaf of bread

hamburger buns

hot dog buns

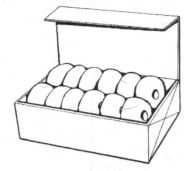
a dozen doughnuts

a dozen cookies

Let's Talk: It's an Apple Pie

Baker: Good morning, Mrs. Lee. May I help you today?

Mrs. Lee: Yes, please. What kind of pie is this?

Baker: It's an apple pie.

Mrs. Lee: Are those chocolate chip cookies?

Baker: Yes, they are.

Mrs. Lee: I'd like an apple pie and a dozen chocolate chip cookies.

☛ **Practice: "What kind of bread is this?"**

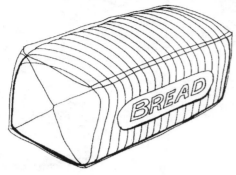

1. S1: What kind of bread is this?
   S2: It's white bread.

2. S1: What kind of cake is that?
   S2: It's a chocolate cake.

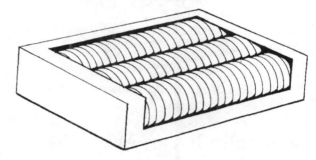

3. S1: Are those hamburger buns?
   S2: Yes, they are.

4. S1: Are these chocolate chip cookies?
   S2: No, they aren't.

☛ **Practice: "May I help you today?"**

1. S1: May I help you today?

   S2: Yes, please. I'd like a dozen doughnuts and a loaf of bread.

   S1: Okay. A dozen doughnuts and a loaf of bread.

2. S1: May I help you?

   S2: I'd like a lemon cake and a package of hamburger buns, please.

   S1: Okay, a lemon cake and a package of hamburger buns.

★ **Something Extra:** Cakes for Special Occasions

a cake
for a birthday

a cake
for a wedding

a cake
for a graduation

Let's Talk: I'd Like a Cake for Saturday

Maria: I'd like a cake for Saturday.
It's for a graduation.

Baker: What kind of cake?

Maria: A lemon cake, please.

Baker: Okay. A lemon cake for Saturday.

☛ **Practice Activity**

Practice ordering a cake for a special occasion.

S1: I'd like a cake for _Monacday_
It's for a _gradyaion_

S2: What kind of cake?

S1: A _cranbirry_ cake, please.

S2: Okay. A _cranbirry_ cake for _Monday_.

Reading: An Anniversary Celebration

Friday is the 25th wedding anniversary of Alice and Ben Lee. The party is on Saturday. Maria is at the bakery today. She is ordering a lemon cake for the anniversary party. Lemon is Ben's favorite flavor. It is a very large cake. On the cake it says, "Happy Silver Anniversary, Alice and Ben." This is a special cake. It costs $45.00.

Discussion

1. What kind of celebration are the Lees having?
2. What is a "silver" anniversary? What is a "golden" anniversary?
3. What kind of cake is Maria ordering? Why?
4. How much is the cake?
5. Do you have cakes for special occasions? What kinds of celebrations?
6. Do you buy or bake your own cakes?
7. What is your favorite kind of cake?

✎ Writing

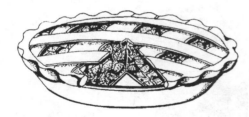

1. S1: What kind _of_ _pie_ this?
   S2: It's an apple pie.

2. S1: _what_ are those?
   S2: _The ya,a they're_ chocolate chip cookies.

3. S1: Is that _a loaf_ of white _bread_ ?
   S2: Yes, _it is_ .

4. S1: May I help you?
   S2: Yes, please. _what is_ that?
   S1: _That is_ a lemon cake.

Lesson 18 Activity Pages

A. Talk about the picture.

HAPPY ANNIVERSARY
Alice and Ben

Happy Silver Anniversary

B. Match the questions and the answers.

1. What kind of party is it? __d__   a. No, they aren't.

2. Are Ben and Alice happy? __e__   b. Yes, it is.

3. Is that an apple pie? __b__   c. It's a lemon cake.

4. What kind of cake is that? __c__   d. It's an anniversary party.

5. Are those muffins? __a__   e. Yes, they are.

C. Look at the picture. Read the conversation and fill in the blanks.

are	is	those	anniversary	kind	lemon	pie	and

Mrs. Gilmore: Oh my! Ben _____ Alice are so happy!

Mr. Chavez: Why not? It's their _____.

Mrs. Gilmore: Yes, 25 years!!

Mrs. Leon: Uh, excuse me. Is that an apple _____?

Mr. Chavez: Yes it _____.

Mrs. Leon: And what kind of cookies are _____?

Mrs. Gilmore: Chocolate chip. They _____ very good!

Mrs. Leon: Oh! Well, what _____ of cake is that?

Mrs. Gilmore: It's a _____ cake.

Mrs. Leon: Hmm, chocolate, apple and lemon. I'd like all 3!

Unit Six Evaluation

I. Listening Comprehension

Listen to the teacher.
Circle the letter of the correct answer, A or B.

1.

A   B

2.
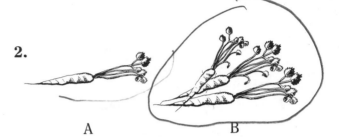
A   B

3.

A. Yes   B. No

4.

A. chocolate chip   B. a dozen

5.

$1.89
A. Yes, it is.
B. No, it isn't.

6.

35¢ EA.   35¢ LB.
A. They're 35 cents each.
B. They're 35 cents a pound.

7.

A. They're doughnuts.
B. They're hamburger buns.

8.

A. They're cookies.
B. They're pies.

II. Reading

Circle the correct answer.

1. Is _____ a grapefruit?

   these   this   those

2. Are _____ carrots?

   this   that   those

3. I'd like a _____ of bread.

   dozen   loaf   pound

4. _____ the fruit salad.

   Cut   Serve   Peel

III. Writing

Choose the correct question or answer
and write it on the line.

Tom: Is this an apple pie?

Ann: _____

Tom: What kind is it?

Ann: _____

Ann: _____

_____

Tom: Yes, they are.

Ann: _____

Tom: They're $1.98 a dozen.

Questions/Answers to Write
Are these chocolate chip cookies?
How much are they?
Is this a doughnut?
It's a cake.
It's a lemon pie.
No, it isn't.
Yes, it is.

Unit Seven

Here, There, and Over There

Where Are the Children?

Objectives: In this lesson you will learn about places in the neighborhood and how to ask and answer questions about where the people are.

✔ Review: A Party

Plan a class party. Plan the food and make a shopping list.

Something New: Places in the Neighborhood
Listen and Look

These are places in our neighborhood.

He's at the bank.

She's at the market.

They're at the post office.

 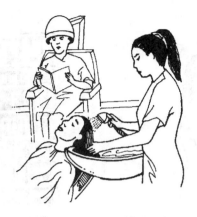 

She's at the laundromat.　　　She's at the beauty shop.　　　He's at the drugstore.

 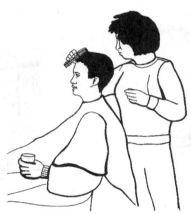 

They're at the video store.　　　He's at the barber shop.　　　She's at the library.

Let's Talk: Where Are the Children?

Tomas is home from work, but the children aren't home yet.

Tomas:　Hi, Sara. I'm home.

Sara:　Hi, Tomas.

Tomas:　Where are the children?

Sara:　They're at the library.

Tomas:　It's late. It's after 5.

Sara:　Please go and get them.

☛ **Practice: "Where's Sara?"**

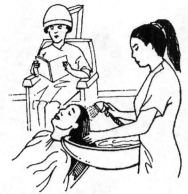

1. S1: Where's Sara?
   S2: She's at the beauty shop.

2. S1: Where's Tomas?
   S2: He's at the video store.

3. S1: Where are the children?
   S2: They're at the market.

4. S1: Is Lisa at the library
      or the market?
   S2: She's at the library.

■ Interaction: Where Am I?

1. One volunteer go to the front of the classroom, choose a picture of a place, and hold it behind your back.

2. Ask and answer questions.

   Example: Volunteer: Where am I?

   Students: Are you at the bank?

   Volunteer: Yes, I am/No, I'm not.

3. The student who guesses correctly will change places with the volunteer.

Something New: Here and There

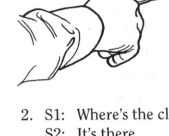

1. S1: Where's the watch?
   S2: It's here.

2. S1: Where's the clock?
   S2: It's there.

3. S1: Where are the waiters?
   S2: They're here.

4. S1: Where's the dishwasher?
   S2: He's there.

5. S1: Where is the teacher?
   S2: She's here.

6. S1: Where are the students?
   S2: They're there.

Let's Talk: At the Library

Tomas is at the library. He is looking for the children. Tomas sees Jane, a neighbor.

Tomas: Are Tom and Lisa here?

Jane: Yes, they are.

Tomas: Where are they?

Jane: Over there. By the magazines.

Tomas: Oh, yes. Thanks, Jane.

☞ **Practice: "He's here"**

1. S1: Where's Tom?
   S2: He's here.

2. S1: Where's Lisa?
   S2: She's there.

☞ **Practice: "By the lemons"**

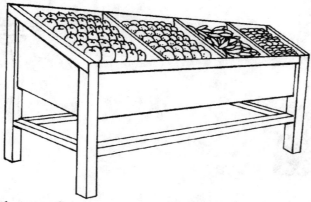

3. S1: Where are the bananas?
   S2: They're over there. By the lemons.

4. S1: Where are the oranges?
   S2: They're here. By the apples.

■ Interaction: Where's Lisa?

1. Five or six students stand in different parts of the room.
2. Ask and answer questions.

    Example: "Where's Lisa?"

    "She's here." or "She's there."

Note: You can also say "She's right here." or "She's over there."

Reading: My Neighborhood

I live in a very convenient neighborhood. There are many stores near my home. I walk to the stores. The children walk to school. My neighborhood is like a small town.

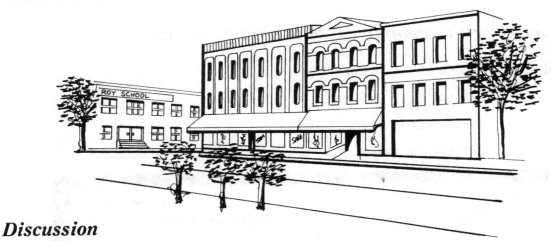

Discussion

1. Where are the stores in your neighborhood?
2. How do the children go to school?
3. Is your neighborhood a convenient place? Why?

✍ Writing

Fill in the missing words:

1. _____ Sara?

2. She's _____ the post office.

3. _____ the post office?

4. It's _____ there.

Lesson 19 Activity Pages

A. Listen and check the correct location.

	the bank	the market	the library	the video store	the laundromat	the post office
1. Tom						
2. Sara						
3. Tony						
4. May						
5. Richard						
6. Maria						

B. Talk about Maria's appointment book with a partner.

Examples: S1: It's Monday. Is Maria at the post office?

S2: Yes, she is.

S1: It's Thursday. Where's Maria?

S2: She's at the market.

January 1993

MONDAY 4 — POST OFFICE, 2 p.m.

TUESDAY 5 — DRUGSTORE, 5:00 p.m.

WEDNESDAY 6 — LIBRARY, 7 p.m.

THURSDAY 7 — MARKET, 4 p.m.

FRIDAY 8 — BANK, 4:30 p.m.

January 1993

SAT. 9 — BEAUTY SHOP, 10 A.M.

SUN. 10 — LAUNDROMAT

C. Now write questions and answers about Maria's appointment book.

1. It's Monday. Is Maria at the post office?_____ *Yes, she is.* _____

2. It's Thursday. Where is Maria?_____.

3. It's Saturday. _____ Maria? _____ at the beauty shop.

4. It's Tuesday. _____ at the drugstore? _____.

5. It's Friday. _____ Maria? She's_____.

6. It's _____. _____ at the library? Yes, _____.

Where's My Wallet?

Objectives: In this lesson you will learn to talk about the locations of objects, using the words *in, on,* and *under.*

✔ Review: Places in the Neighborhood

Nine students pick up pictures and stand in different parts of the room.
Talk about where you see the pictures.

> ***Examples:*** S1: Where's the laundromat?
>
> S2: (student with laundromat picture) It's here.
>
> S1: Where?
>
> S3: (pointing) It's over there.

Something New: My Wallet
Listen and Look

Where is your money?

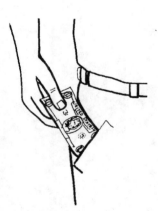

In your wallet?   In your handbag/purse?   In your pocket?

My money is in my wallet.

Bills are in my wallet.

Coins are in my wallet.

My identification cards are in my wallet.

My Social Security card is in my wallet.

My driver's license is in my wallet.

My wallet is on the table.

My handbag/purse is under the table.

☛ **Practice: "It's in my wallet"**

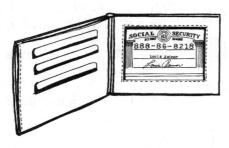

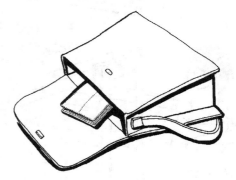

1. S1: Where's your Social Security card?
   S2: It's in my wallet.

2. S1: Where's your wallet?
   S2: It's in my purse.

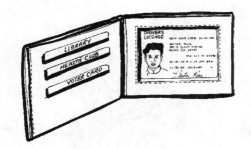

3. S1: Where are your ID cards?
   S2: They're in my wallet.

4 S1: Are your coins in your wallet?
  S2: Yes, they are.

5. S1: Where's your wallet?
   S2: It's on the table.

6. S1: Where's your handbag?
   S2: It's under the table.

Let's Talk: Where's My Wallet?

It's time for a coffee break. The food truck is outside. May is looking for her wallet.

Tony: Let's go, May. The food truck is here.

May: Just a minute, Tony.

Tony: What's the matter?

May: Where's my wallet? It isn't in my handbag.

Tony: There it is. It's under your bag.

May: Oh, thank goodness! Here it is.

☞ Practice: "Here it is"

1. S1: Where's your driver's license?
   S2: Here it is. It's in my wallet.

2. S1: Where's my handbag?
   S2: There it is. It's on the floor.

■ Interaction: Is It in the Purse?

1. One volunteer go to the front of the classroom and secretly hide an item (wallet, ID card, dollar bill, dime) in, on, or under a wallet or purse.

2. Ask and answer questions to guess where the item is.

   Examples:

S1:	Is it in the purse?
Volunteer:	No, it isn't.
S2:	Is it under the purse?
Volunteer:	No, it isn't.

3. The student who guesses correctly will change places with the volunteer.

Reading: What's in the Bag?

What's in May's bag? Let's look.

wallet
keys
mirror
lipstick
gum
pen
pencil
coins
letter
glasses

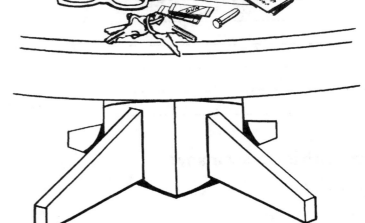

Discussion

1. What's in your handbag? What's in your pocket?
2. What items do women carry?
3. What items do men carry?
4. What items do both men and women carry?

✍ Writing

1. Look at the list of things in May's bag.
2. Make a list of the things in your bag, wallet, or pocket.

_____

_____

_____

_____

_____

_____

_____

_____

_____

_____

_____

_____

_____

_____

_____

_____

_____

_____

☞ Practice Activity: How many?

1. Form groups of 3 or 4.
2. Look at everyone's lists.
   Ask "How many things are on your list?"
3. See who has the largest number of items.
4. See who has the smallest number.

Lesson 20 Activity Pages

A. Talk about the picture.

B. Look at the picture and write the missing words.

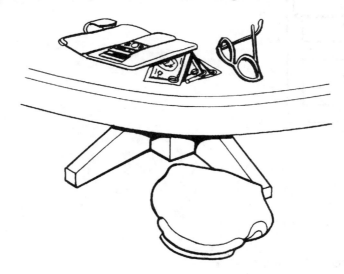

1. The glasses are _____ *on* _____ the table.

2. The purse is _____ the table.

3. The money is _____ the wallet.

4. The wallet is _____ the table.

5. The ID cards are _____ the wallet.

C. Read and do it.

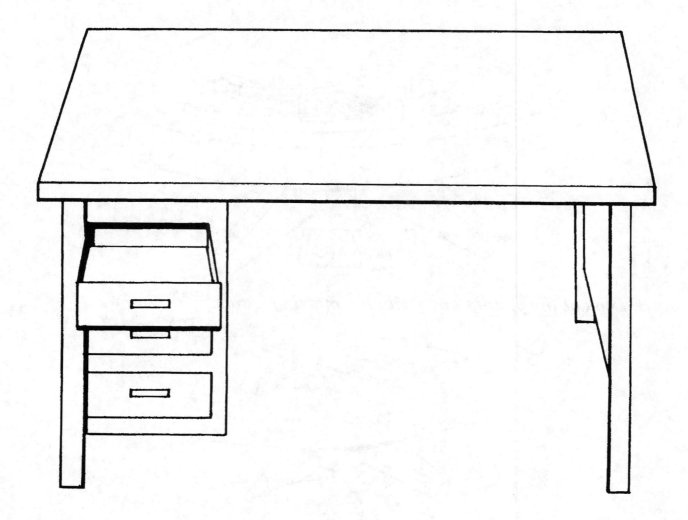

1. Draw a book in the first drawer.

2. Draw a telephone on the desk.

3. Draw a wastebasket under the desk.

4. Draw a notebook by the telephone on the desk.

5. Draw a pencil on the notebook.

D. Look at the pictures. Listen to the conversation.

E. Look at the pictures on page 179 and write the conversation.

Alice: Oh no! Where ____are____ my ____keys____ ?

Ben: They're _____ there, by your wallet.

Alice: No, those _____ my keys, those _____ quarters.

Ben: Oh, they're _____ .

Alice: No, those are _____ .

Ben: Ah, yes. Your keys are there!

Alice: No, _____ a lipstick. Ah–hah! _____ they are.

Ben: Those aren't your keys!

Alice: Yes, they _____! Ben, put on your glasses!

Ben: Oh no! _____?

F. Write three yes/no questions.

Examples: Is Alice happy?
Are the keys in the purse?

1. _____

2. _____

3. _____

Notes

Lesson 21

Let's Cook Dinner!

Objectives: In this lesson you will learn about the kitchen. You will also make and follow requests.

✔ Review: What's in My Pocket?

1. One student go to the front of the classroom and ask:
   "What's in my bag/pocket? Guess."

2. Ask your partner about keys, wallet, etc.

   S1: Where are your keys?

   S2: They're in my pocket.

   S1: Where's her wallet?

   S2: It's in her bag.

Something New: Rosa's Kitchen
Listen and Look

This is Rosa's kitchen.

1. This is a stove.

2. This is a counter.
   These are counters.

3. This is a cabinet.
   These are cabinets.

4. This is a sink.

5. This is a refrigerator.

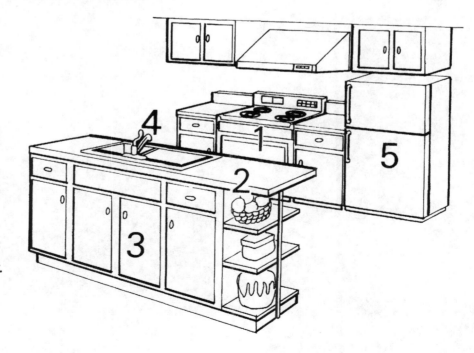

☛ **Practice: "It's a stove"**

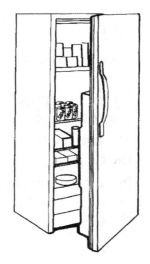

1. S1: What's this?
   S2: It's a stove.

2. S1: What's that?
   S2: It's a refrigerator.

☛ **Practice: "What are these?"**

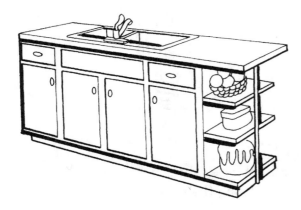

3. S1: What are these?
   S2: They're cabinets.

4. S1: What are those?
   S2: They're counters.

■ **Interaction:** What's in Your Kitchen?

Talk to your partner or group about the items in your kitchen.

Example: S1: What's in your kitchen?
S2: A stove, a refrigerator, etc.

Let's Talk: Let's Cook Dinner!

Rosa and Linda have just come home from the market.

Rosa: Please put the carrots in the refrigerator.

Linda: All right, mother. And the cabbage?

Rosa: Put it on the counter, please. Next to the stove.

Linda: Okay.

Rosa: Thanks, Linda. Now let's cook dinner!

☞ Practice: "It's on the counter"

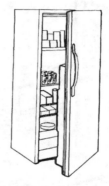

1. S1: Where's the cabbage?
   S2: It's on the counter.

2. S1: Where's the soda?
   S2: It's in the refrigerator.

☞ Practice: "They're next to the cabbage"

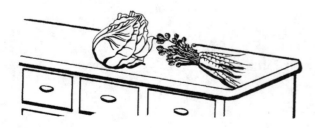

3. S1: Where are the carrots?
   S2: They're next to the cabbage.

4. S1: Where's the stove?
   S2: It's next to the cabinet.

■ Interaction: Put the Carrots on the Counter

1. Draw a kitchen on the chalkboard.
2. Volunteers go to the board and draw items. Students tell them where to put the items.

   Examples:

   S1: Put the **carrots** on the **counter**.

   S2: Put the **cabbage** in the **sink**.

Reading: Rosa's Living Room

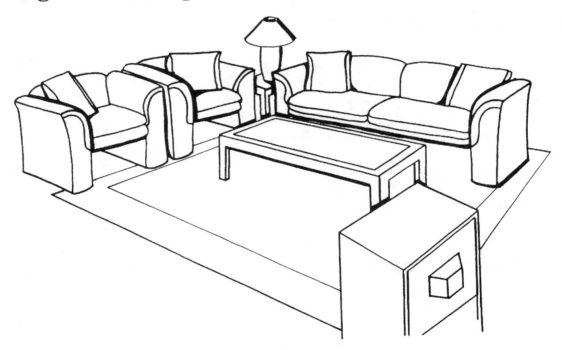

This is Rosa's living room. There is a sofa in the room. There are two chairs and a TV set in the room. A coffee table is in front of the sofa. A table is next to the sofa. There is a lamp on it. A rug is on the floor. It is a comfortable room.

Discussion

1. Where is the lamp?
2. What's in front of the sofa?
3. What's next to the sofa?
4. Do you think Rosa's living room is a comfortable room? Why?

✎ Writing

1. Fill in the missing words.

under	on	in front of	sofa	kitchen	living

   a. The coffee table is _____ the sofa.

   b. A rug is _____ the floor.

   c. There is a _____ in the room.

   d. Rosa's _____ room is comfortable.

2. List five items in a kitchen.

   _____

   _____

   _____

   _____

   _____

3. List five items in a living room.

   _____

   _____

   _____

   _____

   _____

Lesson 21 Activity Page

A. Read and answer the questions. Ask your partner the questions.

1. Where is your ID card? _____ .

2. Is your money in your pocket or in your wallet? _____ .

3. Is your money in a bank? _____ .

4. Is your home near a bank? _____ .

5. Is your home near a market? _____ .

B. BINGO!

- Walk around the room and ask your classmates "*Are you...*" questions.
- Classmates who answer yes write their first names in the boxes.
- When you have four names in a row—across, down, or from corner to corner—shout *BINGO!*

_____ from Mexico	_____ from Japan	_____ from China	_____ from El Salvador
_____ in the kitchen at 7:30 a.m.	_____ in the kitchen at 6:00 p.m.	_____ in the classroom at 9:00 a.m.	_____ in the living room at 10:00 p.m.
_____ at the bank on Fridays	_____ at the market on Thursdays	_____ at the laundromat on Sundays	_____ at the market on Saturdays
_____ a student	_____ from the U.S.	_____ at the bank on Saturdays	_____ in the classroom at 7:00 p.m.

Notes

Unit Seven Evaluation

I. Listening Comprehension

Listen to the teacher. Circle the correct answer, A or B.

1.

A　　　　　B

2.

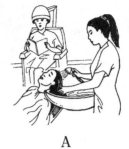

A　　　　　B

3.

A　　　　　B

4.

A　　　　　B

5.

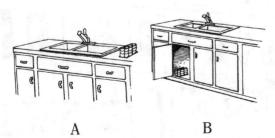

A　　　　　B

6.

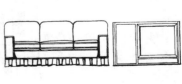

A　　　　　B

II. Reading

Circle the correct answer.

1. He's _____ the bank.

    is   at   to

2. She's at the beauty _____.

    store   office   shop

3. Put the cabbage _____ the counter.

    in   on   at

4. Where is the bag of groceries?

She's here.   It's here.   It's there.

III. Writing

Choose the correct word and write it on the line.

Where	on	there	Is	at	Where's	under	Next to	isn't

1. _____ May here?

2. No, she _____.

3. _____ is she?

4. She's _____ the laundromat.

5. _____ the laundromat?

6. It's over _____.

_____ the bank.

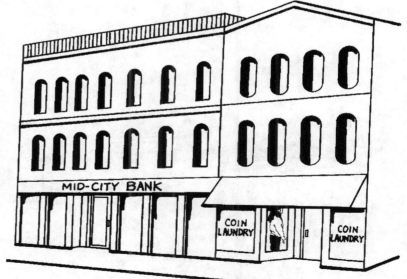

190

Delta's Apple Pie, Book 1A

Unit Eight

Family Ties

He's My Son

Objectives: In this lesson you will learn to ask and answer questions about families.

✔ Review: In, On, Under

Ask each other about locations of keys, wallets, notebooks, coins, bills, combs, etc.

Example: Where are your keys?

They're in my pocket.

Something New: The Kim Family
Listen and Look

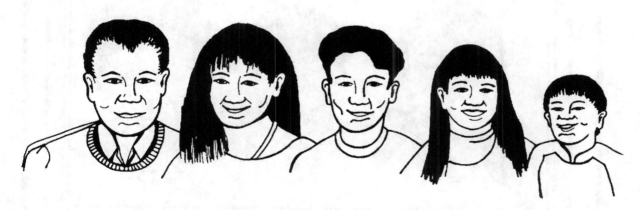

Mr. and Mrs. Kim   Joe Kim   Lucy Kim   Henry Kim

☛ Practice: "Who is he?"

Don Kim   Jae Kim

1. S1: Who is he?
   S2: He's Don Kim.
       He's Jae's husband.
   S1: Who is she?
   S2: She's Jae Kim.
       She's Don's wife.
   S1: Mr. and Mrs. Kim are
       husband and wife.

Joe Kim   Lucy Kim

2. S1: Who is he?
   S2: He's Joe Kim.
       He's Lucy's brother.
   S1: Who is she?
   S2: She's Lucy Kim.
       She's Joe's sister.
   S1: Joe and Lucy are brother and sister.

Mrs. Kim   Lucy

3. S1: Who's Mrs. Kim?
   S2: She's the mother (of the family).
   S1: Who's she?
   S2: She's Lucy. She's the daughter.

Mr. Kim   Joe

4. S1: Who's Mr. Kim?
   S2: He's the father (of the family).
   S1: Who's he?
   S2: He's Joe. He's a son.

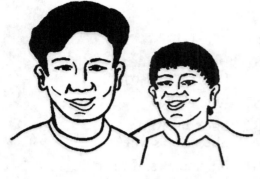

Joe   Henry

5. S1: Who are they?
   S2: They're Joe and Henry Kim.
   S1: Are they brothers?
   S2: Yes, they are.

Henry   Lucy

6. S1: Who are they?
   S2: They're Lucy and Henry Kim.
   S1: Are they brother and sister?
   S2: Yes, they are.

Don   Jae   Joe   Lucy   Henry

7. S1: Is this the Kim family?
   S2: Yes it is. Jae and Don Kim are the parents, and
       Joe, Lucy, and Henry are the children.

Let's Talk: He's My Son

Jim Garcia is showing his friend a photo of his family.

Jim Garcia: This is my wife. Her name's Maria.

Jae Kim: Who's he?

Jim: That's Peter. He's my son.

Jae: Is she your daughter?

Jim: Yes, she is. Her name's Gina.

☛ **Practice: "He's Jae's husband"**

1. S1: Who is Don Kim?
   S2: He's Jae Kim's husband.

2. S1: Who is Don Kim?
   S2: He's Lucy's father.

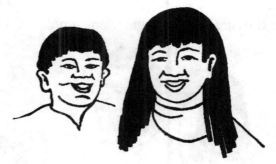

3. S1: Who is Henry Kim?
   S2: He's Mr. and Mrs. Kim's son.

4. S1: Who is Henry Kim?
   S2: He's Lucy's brother.

5. S1: Who is Lucy Kim?
   S2: She is Mr. Kim's daughter.

6. S1: Who is Lucy Kim?
   S2: She's Joe's sister.

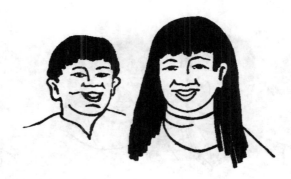

7. S1: Is Lucy Mrs. Kim's mother?
   S2: No, she isn't. She's her daughter.

8. S1: Is Henry Lucy's brother?
   S2: Yes, he is.

196

☛ Practice Activity: Introduce the Kim family

1. Five students (2 women and 3 men) come to the front of the class to play members of the Kim family.
2. One student introduce members of his/her "family" to the class.

   Example: "I am Joe Kim. This is my mother. Her name's Jae Kim. This is my father. His name's Don Kim, etc."
3. Another student introduce the family, too.

Reading: Saturday Morning

It is Saturday morning at the Kim house. Lucy and her brother Joe are in the kitchen. Her mother is in the bedroom. Her brother Henry is in the living room. Her father isn't there. He's at work.

Discussion

1. What day is it?
2. Where are the members of the Kim family?
3. Where are you on Saturday mornings?
4. Where is your brother/sister/husband/wife on Saturday mornings?

✍ Writing

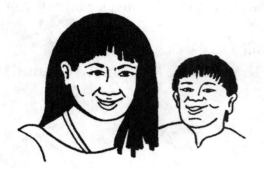

1. Is Mrs. Kim Henry's mother?

   _____ .

2. Who is Don Kim?

   _____

   _____

   _____ .

3. Who is Joe?

   _____

   _____

   _____ .

4. Is Lucy Don Kim's wife?

   _____ .

★ **Something Extra:** My Family

Draw a picture of your family: husband, wife, mother, father, brothers, sisters, children.

Write about your family.

This is my family.

Lesson 22 Activity Pages

A. Listen and name the family members.

The Gonzalez Family

| Hector | Vera | Betty | Chris |

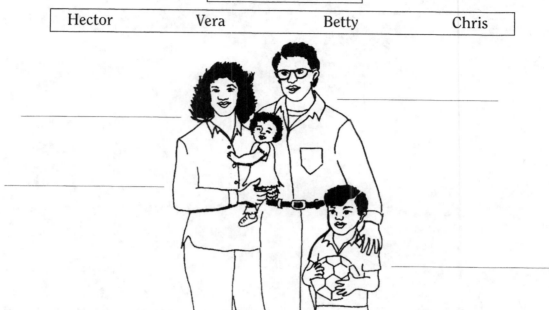

B. Look at the picture. Read the answers and write the questions.

1. *Is Hector Gonzalez the father?*

   Yes, he is the father.

2. _____?

   Yes, she is the mother.

3. _____?

   She's the daughter.

4. _____?

   He's the son.

5. _____?

   No, they are the parents.

6. _____?

   Yes, they are the children.

C. Look at the picture and write the missing words in the story.

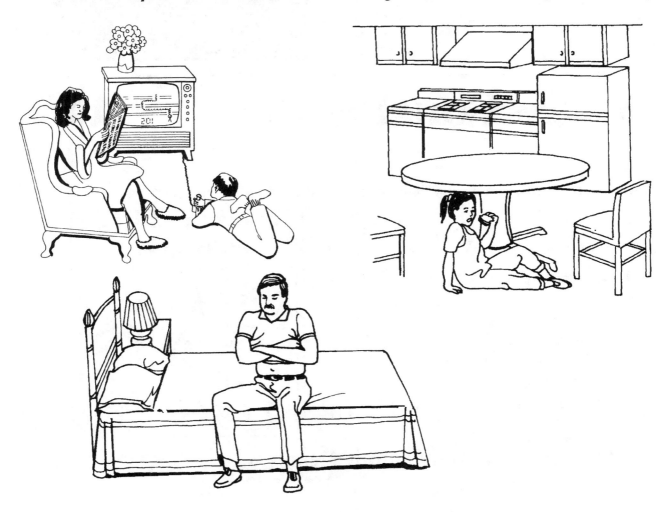

This is my family. I'm Ivan Petrov. Today is Sunday and my family is at home. My

_____, Ivana, is in the living room with my _____ Georgie.

My _____ Ivan, Sr., is in the bedroom. He's _____ the bed. My

_____, Janet, is in the _____. She's under the table with her

sandwich. And where am I? I'm not _____. I'm at the video store. Sunday

night is a good night for a movie!

We're Cousins

Objectives: In this lesson you will learn to ask and answer more questions about families.

✔ Review: Family

1. Look at the picture of the Kim family.

   (It's Lucy Kim's family. She's the daughter.)

2. Tell your partner about everyone in Lucy's family.

3. Tell your partner about your family.

Something New: More Family Members
Listen and Look

Jim Garcia and his family

Jim, his wife Maria, his son Peter, and his daughter Gina

Victor Garcia and his family

Victor, his wife Sonia, his daughters Luisa and Cecilia

Jim Garcia and Victor Garcia are brothers.

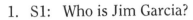 **Practice: "He's Luisa's uncle"**

1. S1: Who is Jim Garcia?
    S2: He's Luisa's uncle.
    S1: Who is Maria?
    S2: She's Luisa's aunt.

2. S1: Who is Victor?
    S2: He's Peter's uncle.
    S1: Who is Sonia?
    S2: She's Peter's aunt.

3. S1: Who is Luisa?
    S2: She's Jim's niece.

4. S1: Who is Peter?
    S2: He's Victor's nephew.

5. S1: Are Gina and Cecilia sisters?
    S2: No, they aren't. They're cousins.

6. S1: Who is Cecilia?
    S2: She's Peter's cousin.

Let's Talk: We're Cousins

Peter and Luisa Garcia are students in Mrs. Baker's class.

Mrs. Baker: Luisa, are you and Peter brother and sister?

Luisa: No, we aren't. We're cousins.

Peter: That's right. Her father and my father are brothers.

Mrs. Baker: You are related! I thought so!

☛ **Practice: "Are you related?"**

1. S1: Are you related?
   S2: Yes, we are. We're sisters.

2. S1: Are you related?
   S2: Yes, we are. We're cousins.

3. S1: Are they related?
   S2: Yes, they are. They're brother and sister.

4. S1: Are you related?
   S2: No, we aren't. We're friends.

☞ **Practice: "He's my uncle"**

5. S1: Is he your father?
    S2: No, he isn't. He's my uncle.

6. S1: Who is she?
    S2: She's my aunt.

7. S1: Is Peter Garcia your son?
    S2: No, he isn't. He's my nephew.

8. S1: Is Cecilia your niece?
    S2: Yes, she is.

■ **Interaction:** Talk about Families

1. Tell your partner about your aunts and uncles.
2. How many are on your mother's side of the family?
3. How many are on your father's side of the family?
4. How many cousins are there?

Reading: The Kim Family

Don Kim is from a large family. In his father's family there are six children. There are three daughters and three sons. Two sons are the first and second children. Don is the third child. His three sisters are the fourth, fifth, and sixth children.

In Don's family there are three children. His son Joe is 16 years old. His daughter Lucy is his second child. She is 13. His son Henry is 7.

☛ Practice Activity

1. Draw a picture (or chart) of Don Kim and his brothers and sisters. Put them in order. Write Don's name on his picture.

2. Draw a picture of Don's children. Put their names and their ages on the pictures.

3. In your family are you the first, second, third, fourth child? Where are you in your family? Draw yourself and your brothers and sisters.

✍ Writing

1. Is Victor Peter's father?

   No, he isn't. _____

   _____ .

2. Who is Cecilia?

   _____

   _____ .

3. Are Peter and Luisa related?

   _____ .

   _____ cousins .

4. _____

   _____ ?

   Yes, they are. They're sisters.

5. Is Sonia Peter's cousin?

   _____ .

   _____ .

6. Who is Jim?

   _____

   _____ .

Lesson 23 Activity Page

A. Put the words in pairs. Write the words for men on the left. Write the words for women on the right.

uncle
husband
daughter
nephew
aunt
mother
son
niece
brother
wife
father
sister

Men

father

Women

mother

B. Look at the family tree and answer the questions.

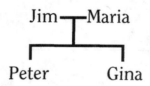

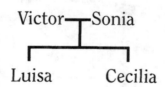

1. Who is Sonia's husband?

2. Who is Jim's wife?

3. Who are Cecilia's cousins?

4. Who is Gina's aunt?

5. Who is Luisa's father?

6. Who is Victor's nephew?

7. Who is Victor's brother?

8. Who are Jim's nieces?

9. Who are Luisa and Cecilia's parents?

10. Who are Peter's aunt and uncle?

Notes

He's at Work

Objective: In this lesson you will learn to use the expressions: *at home, at work, at school.*

✔ **Review:** Are You Related?

How many people are there in your class with the same family name? Are they related? Ask your classmates if they're related.

Example: Gina, are you and Cecilia related?
Yes, we are. We're cousins.

Fill in the information on the chart. The example has been done for you.

Family (Last) Name	First Name #1	First Name #2	No	Yes	How?
1. *Garcia*	*Gina*	*Cecilia*		*X*	*cousins*
2.					
3.					
4.					

Something New: At Work and At Home
Listen and Look

She's at work.

He's at home.

They're at school.

Let's Talk: Is Your Husband at Home?

Mrs. Kim: Hello.

Mrs. Jones: Hello, Mrs. Kim. This is Mrs. Jones. Is your husband at home?

Mrs. Kim: I'm sorry, he isn't.

Mrs. Jones: Is he at work?

Mrs. Kim: Yes, he is.

Mrs. Jones: I'll call back later. Thank you. Goodbye.

☛ **Practice: "This is Mrs. Kim"**

1. S1: Hello.
   S2: Hello, Jim. This is Mrs. Kim.
       Is your wife at home?
   S1: Yes, she is. Just a minute.

2. S1: Hello.
   S2: Hello, Mrs. Garcia.
       Is Gina at home?
   S1: No, she isn't. She's at school.

3. S1: Where is he?
   S2: He's at work.

4. S1: Where are they?
   S2: They're at school.

Let's Review: At Work and At Home

Mrs. Kim isn't at home. She's at work.
She's at the hospital.

Mr. Kim isn't at work. He's at home.
He's in the living room.

Joe and Sally are at school.
Joe is in the classroom.
Sally is on the playground.

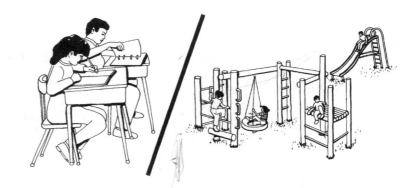

☛ **Practice: "She's at work"**

1. S1: Where is Mrs. Kim?
   S2: She's at work.

2. S1: Where are Joe and Lucy?
   S2: They're at school.

3. S1: Is Mr. Kim at home?
   S2: Yes, he is.
   S1: Where is he?
   S2: He's in the living room.

4. S1: Are Mr. and Mrs. Kim at home?
   S2: Mr. Kim is at home.
       Mrs. Kim isn't.
   S1: Where is Mrs. Kim?
   S2: She's at work.
       She's at the hospital.

5. S1: Is Sally at school?

   S2: Yes, she is.

   S1: Is she in the classroom?

   S2: No, she isn't. She's on the playground.

■ Interaction: At Home, School, and Work

In small groups, ask other students about their families. Use "at home," "at school," and "at work" to talk about where your family members are.

> *Example:* S1: Is your husband at home?
>
> S2: No, he isn't.
>
> S1: Where is he?
>
> S2: He's at work.

Reading: On the Telephone

Ana Silva is on the telephone. Her son Paul is calling. Paul is away at school in another city.

Paul: Hi, Mom.

Ana: Paul. Where are you? Are you at school?

Paul: No, I'm not. I'm here in the city. I'm at the bus station. Please pick me up.

Ana: Oh, okay. Be there in 30 minutes.

Paul: All right. See you in a half hour.

Discussion

1. Is Paul in another city?

2. Where is he?

3. Is Ana at home?

4. Are members of your family in other cities? Where are they?

✍ Writing

1. Is he at home?

   _____ .

2. _____

   _____ ?

   Yes, she is.

3. Where are they?

   _____

   _____ .

4. Are they at home?

   _____ .

   Where are they?

   _____

   _____ .

Lesson 24 Activity Pages

A. Talk about the pictures.

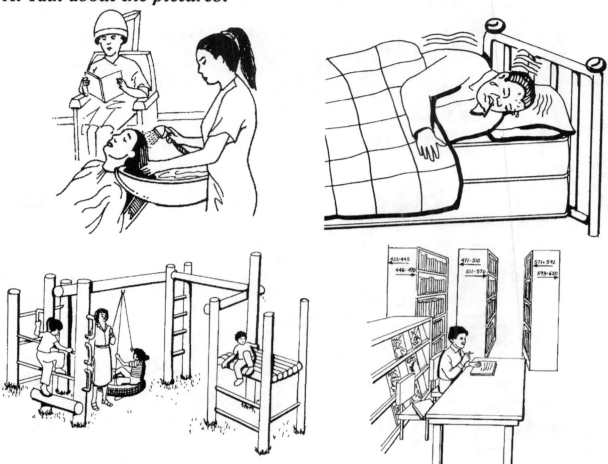

B. Look at the pictures and write the answers to the questions.

1. Is Mrs. Lee at home?

   No, she isn't.

2. Is Sally Lee on the playground?

   _____.

3. Where is Sally's father?

   _____.

4. Where is Sally's teacher?

   _____.

5. Is Sam Lee at home?

   _____.

6. Where is he?

   _____.

C. Write your information and then ask your partner.

1. What is your name? _____ .

2. Where are you from? _____ .

3. Are you a student or a teacher? _____ .

4. Are you at school in the evening? _____ .

5. Are you at home in the morning? _____ .

6. Where are you in the morning? _____

_____ .

7. Where are you at 6:00 in the evening? _____

_____ .

8. Where are you at 9:30 at night? _____

_____ .

Notes

Unit Eight Evaluation

I. Listening Comprehension

Listen to the teacher. Circle the correct answer, A or B.

1.

A   B

2.

A   B

3.

A   B

4.

A   B

5.

A   B

6.

A   B

7.

A. at home   B. at work

8.

A. He's at school.   B. They're at school.

219

II. Reading

Circle the correct answer.

1. He's the _____.

   mother   sister   son

2. He isn't at home. He's _____.

   at work   living room   bank

3. Are you _____?

   brother   sister   related

4. Jae is _____ wife.

   Don   her   Don's

5. Mr. and Mrs. Kim are the parents, and
   Joe, Lucy, and Henry are the _____.

   brothers   sons   children

6. This is Peter's family.
   This is _____ mother.

   her   Garcia   his

III. Writing

Choose the correct word and write it on the line.

The Garcia Family

This is Cecilia Garcia. These are _____ parents. Her mother's _____ is Sonia,

and her _____ name is Victor. This is her _____. Her name is _____.

brother   father's   her   Luisa   name   sister

Notes

Notes